Summary of

Team of Teams

by General Stanley McChrystal

Instaread

Please Note

This is key takeaways & analysis.

Table of Contents

Overview

Team of Teams by General Stanley McChrystal is an examination of the process he began of restructuring the Joint Special Operations Command management style, from a rigid command structure to a cooperative team comprised of smaller specialized teams. While fighting Al-Qaeda in Iraq (AQI), General McChrystal noted how the United States and coalition militaries were efficient war-fighting machines, but they were not adaptable or effective against the seemingly disordered AQI. In 2005, after a particularly destructive terrorist attack at the opening of a sewage plant near Baghdad, McChrystal began considering whether the efficient structure was actually hindering the counterinsurgency, preventing them from responding to threats in real time and delaying the capture of AQI leader Abu Musab al-Zarqawi.

Modern military management originated at the 1900 World's Fair, when Frederick Winslow Taylor revealed his work in steel production efficiency. Taylor believed that there is a right way to do any given thing, and he built reductionist processes to streamline how production employees work and what they need to know to do their jobs. In reductionist management schemes, employees focus only on their role and need not communicate with other employees or ask questions of their managers about the bigger picture.

Taylor's ideas reconfigured the world of work and entered soldiers' lives in the rigorous routines they must perform, their uniforms and supplies, and their inability to question their superiors or participate in decision-making processes. Lack of communication and involvement of the key operation participants in decision-making were identified as contributing factors in the failure to prevent the September 11, 2001 terrorist attacks on the World Trade Center towers in New York City and in the intelligence backlog between operators and analysts in Iraq.

Taking Navy SEAL training and successful team-building programs at Brigham and Women's Hospital in Boston and other organizations as his models, McChrystal describes the principles of building a team of teams with a common purpose, awareness, and empowerment in an environment where increased data availability and unpredictability arising from complexity seem to reward more hands-on command management styles.

Important People

General Stanley McChrystal: Stanley McChrystal was a four-star general in the United States Army, commander of the International Security Assistance Force, commander of the US Forces Afghanistan, and director of the Joint Staff. He wrote *Team of Teams* about his work to create a more adaptable, effective Joint Special Operations Command during the fight against Al-Qaeda in Iraq.

Tantum Collins: Tantum Collins is a graduate student and Marshall Scholar at the University of Cambridge. He took a course taught by McChrystal at Yale University as an undergraduate and participated in writing and researching *Team of Teams.*

David Silverman: David Silverman is the chief executive officer of CrossLead, a consultancy he co-founded with McChrystal. He was a US Navy SEAL officer, was deployed six times, and participated in writing and researching *Team of Teams.*

Chris Fussell: Chris Fussell is a partner at McChrystal's consultancy, CrossLead, formerly a US Navy SEAL officer who served as an aide to McChrystal at the Joint Special Operations Command. Fussell participated in writing and researching *Team of Teams.*

Abu Musab al-Zarqawi: Abu Musab al-Zarqawi was the leader of Al-Qaeda in Iraq from 2004 until 2006, when he was killed in a bombing directed by McChrystal's Joint Special Operations Command.

Frederick Winslow Taylor: Frederick Winslow Taylor was a mechanical engineer who pioneered efficiency methods and data-driven scientific management during the early 1900s. His concepts became the worldwide standard in management for production.

Tarek al-Tayleb Mohamed Bouazizi: Mohamed Bouazizi was a fruit vendor in Tunisia who protested official corruption and harassment by self-immolating in public in 2010. The incident and subsequent protests of sympathetic activists set into motion the Tunisian Revolution and Arab Spring movements.

Admiral Horatio Nelson: Horatio Nelson was a flag officer of the British Royal Navy until his death in 1805. Nelson was known for his unconventional battle tactics.

George Mueller: George Mueller was the US National Aeronautics and Space Administration's associate administrator of the Office of Manned Space Flight in the 1960s as NASA worked toward the goal of a manned mission to the moon.

Michael Bloomberg: Michael Bloomberg is the founder and chief executive officer of financial data company Bloomberg LP, former mayor of New York City, and multibillionaire. His bullpen management style is similar to that advocated by McChrystal.

Key Takeaways

1. An efficient system is not necessarily effective, especially if the output of the system is not what is needed or it does not make use of the inputs available. Creating an effective system can sometimes reduce its efficiency.

2. The reductionist approach to management revolutionized engineering and spread to other, non-production tasks. However, reductionist management does not work in every scenario.

3. Many processes in the world today are more complex than they were before the information age, making them highly unpredictable and making a reductionist management style less effective. Reduction is still effective in complicated systems, which are more predictable than complex ones.

4. A robust system is effective at countering a specific obstacle, but a resilient system can adapt to unexpected obstacles. A robust system can be fragile if it is not also resilient, and making a resilient system may mean reducing the system's efficiency at countering the threat against which it was designed.

5. A team needs a sense of purpose and trust between members above all to successfully accomplish more than a single person could alone.

6. Creating successful teams can still result in difficulties if different teams do not trust each other. A team of teams consists of cohesive, specialized groups that trust each other to do their jobs and communicate throughout a task.

7. The physical layout of working space can encourage or discourage collaboration and communication. Cubicles and individual offices encourage isolation and territoriality, while open floor plans allow employees to see each other, talk casually, and trust one another.

8. Organization members that do not trust each other do not share information and resent sharing limited resources. Members of teams that trust each other share information and willingly give up access to resources when they know it will benefit the organization's common purpose.

9. The role of a leader in a team of teams is more similar to that of a gardener than the traditional self-confident, omnipotent commander. Leaders who resist the urge to monitor and instruct, and who leave decisions to those further down the chain of command, get equally good decisions and a more efficient organization.

Analysis

Key Takeaway 1

An efficient system is not necessarily effective, especially if the output of the system is not what is needed or it does not make use of the inputs available. Creating an effective system can sometimes reduce its efficiency.

Analysis

It seems that a manager's goal should be to create an effective system first, and that efficiency will follow with time to tweak the processes or find motivated employees. However, legacy systems adapted to a new situation or repurposed for a new output may still seek efficiency even as it loses effectiveness. When a system designed to take in pizza ingredients and produce pizzas is altered to take in pie ingredients and produce pies, retaining processes that made good pizzas, but reduces the quality of pies, or it can overlook opportunities for increased quality or efficiency in pie-making, even if the system produces pie just as quickly as it produced pizza.

Armies of the world have discovered that, with the rise of non-state actors, war today does not resemble the state-driven wars of the past where leaders relied on the support of their citizens and utilized treaties and negotiations. However, the modern army still relies on processes developed prior to the counterinsurgency focus. Just as snipers revolutionized the battlefield during the US Revolutionary War, because no one had considered hiding soldiers in trees rather than lining them up in ranks, war innovators have a considerable advantage over their opponents. The other side is burdened with searching for a solution to the new ideas and also slowly developing their own innovations.

Key Takeaway 2

The reductionist approach to management revolutionized engineering and spread to other, non-production tasks. However, reductionist management does not work in every scenario.

Analysis

Reductionist management is best suited to tasks that must be completed repeatedly, the same way every time, as quickly as possible. Any job that can be reduced to a list of instructions is well-suited to this management style, where workers are not expected to communicate with their colleagues, form a team, or ask questions of their supervisors. For example, on a factory assembly line there is no need for a worker to think of every door installed on a car differently. Uniformity is valued over creativity. Efficiency is the primary goal because the instructions ensure that the process is effective, taking the appropriate inputs, and generating the appropriate outputs. A task, like putting a door on a car, could possibly be done by a robot given the same list of instructions. However, sometimes humans cannot be replaced by robots on the factory floor because of limitations in the design of robots.

By comparison, there are many jobs that cannot be reduced to a set of instructions, and no one would want them managed in a reductionist way, such as doctors and lawyers. For them, efficiency means nothing if a doctor is not effective. While a lawyer may have a set procedure for every court case, starting with meeting the client and moving on to which motions to file in court, that procedure does not resemble a reductionist instruction list. A doctor who treated every patient identically or a lawyer who treated every case identically would not be effective because what their jobs really entail is creativity and adaptive thinking. They need a holistic view of the case at hand to make those decisions, and would not be effective if their knowledge in the field is so narrow as to leave them oblivious if a case does not go as planned.

Key Takeaway 3

Many processes in the world today are more complex than they were before the information age, making them highly unpredictable and making a reductionist management style less effective. Reduction is still effective in complicated systems, which are more predictable than complex ones.

Analysis

The difference between a complicated system and a complex one is the difference between a car and ocean currents. In theory, a car should work if all the parts are in working order, and failure of one part, like a fuse, has a predictable effect on the car, like the interior lights failing. Diagnosing a car can be difficult because the systems are interconnected and some parts are difficult to see, but the range of inputs that impact its functioning are limited, and the outputs are predictable.

On the other hand, ocean currents take a knowable set of inputs and their output motions can be predicted, but the range of inputs is so large as to be unmeasurable, making prediction of the output less reliable. Ocean currents can be so complex that, in one circumstance, the path of a herd of whales may change the direction or force of a current and, in another, the same pod of whales will change nothing substantially. As McChrystal points out, a butterfly flapping its wings may cause a hurricane on the other side of the world, but it is known from observation that it does not happen every time a butterfly flaps its wings.

Aside from the difficulty of diagnosing a problem in a car, the process of fixing one is reductionist in nature. A mechanic could be very effective and efficient if they replace every fuse in a given make, model, and year of car the same way. If replacing a fuse does not solve the problem, it would be because the inputs were not accurately assessed and some other system, like the car's dome light, is faulty. And then the mechanic could not go wrong replacing every dome light in a given type of car the same way. A complicated system is predictable because it shows linear results. However, a complex system shows non-linear results. Too many things can impact a complex system for reasons that are often too complicated to understand, such as a butterfly that can cause a hurricane simply by beating its wings. These linear and non-linear results are the difference between complex and complicated systems.

Key Takeaway 4

A robust system is effective at countering a specific obstacle, but a resilient system can adapt to unexpected obstacles. A robust system can be fragile if it is not also resilient, and making a resilient system may mean reducing the system's efficiency at countering the threat against which it was designed.

Analysis

Highly specialized solutions to problems often arise in response to a significant tragedy, described as the never again mentality. And, in some cases, these robust systems are completely necessary, even if they are not resilient. Car airbags are a robust system because they deploy in response to a specific event and generally do their job, which is to inflate rapidly and prevent passengers from being hurt by impact with the car's interior. However, airbags are not resilient. They only inflate where they are placed, do not prevent other types of injury, like whiplash, and sometimes they inflate when a collision has not occurred. Just because airbags are a fragile, robust system does not mean cars should not be made with them. They still save more lives than they take, and removing them would expose people to much greater danger.

No car maker has created a truly resilient collision safety system, but newer cars do come with more resilient systems that better protect passengers or can prevent accidents entirely. These are created by systems working in tandem, starting with more airbags, crumple zones, stronger frames, shatter-proof glass, and seat belts, and in newer cars incorporating rear-view cameras, proximity sensors, and automatic braking for crash avoidance. Cars are not likely to be able to repair themselves or their passengers in the future, so adaptive crash prevention systems come close to as resilient as car safety systems can get.

If a car were designed to prevent only one type of accident, like skidding off the road due to snow, it might have features like permanent snow chains on the tires. However, that would make the car less effective in nearly every other scenario and, in an accident during different weather, those features could cause more damage than if those features were not there. Another example would be the Netherlands' reaction to a flood that happened in 1958. The Rhine River flooded, killing 1,800 people. To prevent a similar disaster, the country constructed the Delta Works, flood walls meant to hold back a new flood. However, flooding again hit the area in 1993 and 1995, but it came from snow melting off the Alps. The flood walls prevented the water from draining. This example shows that some robust systems cause more harm than good when faced with situations other than the one for which they were designed. Reducing the car's efficiency of crash prevention in snow, by making snow chains removable, increases its effective safety in other scenarios.

Key Takeaway 5

A team needs a sense of purpose and trust between members above all to successfully accomplish more than a single person could alone.

Analysis

Team-building has been an organizational concept for a long time already, but in some organizations the message of teamwork is undermined by a message of competition or by a lack of support from supervisors. Common purpose for team members relies on consistent focus on the goal of the team, not of the individual, and many organizations fail to recognize the contradiction when they send groups to team-building seminars and also give incentives to individuals for achieving more than their team members. Wherever the competitive, individual-focused initiative is added, teams break down.

Similarly, organizations that encourage teams to make decisions may also allow the team supervisor to separate themselves from their decision-making process, give the supervisor decisions to make without input from the team, or restrict the information that the supervisor can give to the team. An example of the detriment of giving one person ultimate decision making power over everyone else is the crash of United Airlines Flight 173. In 1978, Flight 173 had landing gear problems. The pilot was warned multiple times by his crew members that fuel was running dangerously low. However, the pilot ignored these warnings, choosing to wait until the ground crew was prepared for their landing. As a result, the pilot allowed the plane to run out of fuel and it crashed. A flight crew must work as a team. Instead, this captain failed to listen to his fellow teammates, possibly believing that it was more important to dictate everyone else's actions and make major decisions on his own.

Creating a team that demonstrates trust and a common sense of purpose is not a reductionist process, and proving that the team has these qualities may not be possible in some cases. Perseverance is demonstrated by the soldiers in the US Navy SEAL training program, Basic Underwater Demolition SEALS training (BUD/S), a six month program required of all aspiring SEALS. This program is one indicator of a successful team because they understand the need to rely on each other to accomplish the goal, and not relying on the team out of pride results in failure for the whole team.

Key Takeaway 6

Creating successful teams can still result in difficulties if different teams do not trust each other. A team of teams consists of cohesive, specialized groups that trust each other to do their jobs and communicate throughout a task.

Analysis

Teams are often restricted in size to ensure maximum trust and strong relationships between members because the human brain is only capable of trusting a limited number of people. This was probably a useful feature in human evolution, where tribes could move more quickly if they were smaller and were better served by defaulting to distrust of other tribes. In large organizations, tribalism appears again when different regional sales teams engage in competition without a management incentive to compete, or when a team of designers displays lack of confidence in the engineers responsible for making their plans viable. Sometimes this insulation happens because organizations do not encourage communication between these separate teams. Once a design is sent to the engineers, the architects do not get to see how the engineers work to implement the designs. Instead, architects are expected to move on to designing the next project and not distract themselves with something outside of their job descriptions.

The European efforts to join the space race are especially demonstrative because the different countries' engineering teams felt an incentive to keep secrets from each other, and that cooperation was a liability. These ideas were motivated by a patriotic feeling as well as economic advantages.

Key Takeaway 7

The physical layout of working space can encourage or discourage collaboration and communication. Cubicles and individual offices encourage isolation and territoriality, while open floor plans allow employees to see each other, talk casually, and trust one another.

Analysis

Open floor plans are a significant trend in startup culture and in any company looking to adapt quickly like a startup. Even small, one- or two-person operations see the benefit of being around peers and having people available for casual conversations, which is one reason coworking spaces have sprung up in a variety of cities. At these spaces, small organizations can rent a desk or cubicle and share resources like printers, kitchens, and lounges. Sometimes coworking spaces will offer interest clubs or recreational sports to encourage connections between renters.

The open floor plan and mobility of work space has served video game company Valve Software well. They recently published their handbook for new employees to share some of their insights into how best to develop strong team workspaces. [1] Valve employees work at rolling desks, and there are outlets available throughout the office rooms, so employees can simply unplug, roll to a new location, and plug in there whenever they need a change.

Teams generally roll their desks together to facilitate communication, but the handbook also encourages new employees looking for interesting projects to roll their desks over next to someone they would like to work with or whose work they admire.

The notion that in-person communication is necessary for problem-solving also gained attention when Marissa Mayer eliminated the option to work from home after she became CEO of the media company Yahoo. Many people criticized her for making the corporate culture less friendly to parents, Mayer being a new parent herself, but management experts found her policy change encouraged "serendipitous interaction" between employees, strengthening connections face to face that could not be developed long-distance and encouraging employees to toss ideas around for longer periods of time.[2]

Key Takeaway 8

Organization members that do not trust each other do not share information and resent sharing limited resources. Members of teams that trust each other share information and willingly give up access to resources when they know it will benefit the organization's common purpose.

Analysis

In a command of teams where teams do not collaborate and their leaders still fit into a rigid command structure, those teams engage in tribalistic distrust of one another and naturally resent when their access to a valuable resource, like vehicles, is restricted in favor of another team. Not being involved in the decision of where the resource would be best put to use, teams would view this resource reassignment as favoritism and have no way of knowing whether the resource was really put to its best possible use. One of the most surprising revelations McChrystal had while reorganizing the Joint Special Operations Command was that when teams were involved in the decision to assign important resources, how the resources were used, and how those resources were beneficial, they were more willing to volunteer to give up resources to other teams. They did so on the assumption that when they needed the resource, the other teams would be willing to give up their own access in return.

In war, information is power, and the natural inclination of leaders is to restrict access to that information as much as possible to prevent a leak. Secrecy cannot be compromised by teamwork because troop movements and limitations are too valuable in enemy hands. But there is value in informing more than just the upper ranks about operations because contextual information about intelligence and about every step of the operation benefits the people charged with making decisions at every level of the war effort.

Key Takeaway 9

The role of a leader in a team of teams is more similar to that of a gardener than the traditional self-confident, omnipotent commander. Leaders who resist the urge to monitor and instruct, and who leave decisions to those further down the chain of command, get equally good decisions and a more efficient organization.

Analysis

Today, it is not uncommon for employees in a company to copy their supervisors on all emails, wear badges that track their movements around offices, and consent to having their computers monitored for internet access, generating enormous volumes of data that are analyzed for efficiency and adherence to company policies. With radio frequency identification, near-field communication, network surveillance, and data analysis technology growing in capability, employers see their opportunities to manage employees more thoroughly than ever before. However, McChrystal urges leaders to do the opposite. He encourages them to watch and communicate, but only intervene when absolutely necessary and allow workers to make decisions without having to get approval all the way up the chain of command.

His guidance is linked to the strength of surveillance technology and communication today. Where previously soldiers conducting reconnaissance hunted for their target on foot for days and struggled to receive updated intelligence or communicate their questions back to analysts, drone surveillance allows an analyst to keep eyes on an operation from beginning to end, follow a target for weeks at a time, get high-resolution, current images to identify the target in person, and see exactly who the operators are apprehending, or whether they are chasing the wrong vehicle. In these cases, it does little good to ask a general whether to apprehend a target. If the leadership has already instructed soldiers to apprehend someone, the drone pilot and analyst have identified them, and the operators clearly have the right person in their sights, the team can quickly determine how best to apprehend the target in the moment, rather than waking up the general for approval.

Just as a gardener chooses the best plant varieties for the soil, sunlight, and water conditions in a part of the garden, leaders' responsibilities can be more managerial than instructive when all they have to do is remove obstacles (weeds and pests) and provide motivation (fertilizer). In doing so, the leader is really cultivating more capable leaders by distributing responsibilities as they are best suited.

Author's Style

Team of Teams is written in the style of a lecture, starting with an anecdote and expanding into the factors that contributed to the anecdote, then the problems presented by the incident, the sources of those problems, and the solution. The narrative winds this way through various historical examples and more recent relevant events. Readers get a front-row view of the fight against AQI inside the Joint Special Operations Command, following McChrystal's decision-making process. McChrystal also describes his personal influences, the people he has worked with, and failed operations alongside successful ones. The descriptions of historical examples, the response of Brigham and Women's Hospital surgical teams, the Boston Marathon Bombings, and the crash of Flight 137, are thorough, well-cited, and descriptive. Overall, the text provides a balance of the advantages of some systems and their drawbacks. There is not much jargon in the text, and any military-specific terms are defined the first time they are used.

Dialogue is easy to follow even when it happened between military officials regarding their operations, which is surprising considering their use of acronyms. The text also includes diagrams that demonstrate McChrystal's messages about organization.

Each of the various chapters highlights either a managerial problem facing McChrystal and the Joint Special Operations Command in Iraq, or an ideal of leadership and teamwork that contributes to the successful operation of teams of teams. The chapters also follow the

command's progress toward the new management scheme chronologically, so they flow into each other without jarring transitions. Since the focus is on the system's failures at the beginning and its successes at the end, the reader sees the gradual process of change and improvement with a neat resolution.

Author's Perspective

Stanley Allen McChrystal is a retired US Army general. McChrystal was Commander of the International Security Assistance Force, commander of the US Forces Afghanistan, and as Director of the Joint Staff. In his new position as a consultant, McChrystal works with companies to implement management structures similar to the one he developed at the Joint Special Operations Command.

~~~~ END OF INSTAREAD ~~~~

References

1. Valve: Handbook for New Employees, March 2012, http://www.valvesoftware.com/company/Valve_Handbook_LowRes.pdf

2. Henn, Steve. "'Serendipitous Interaction Key To Tech Firms' Workplace Design," National Public Radio. 13 March 2013, http://www.npr.org/sections/alltechconsidered/2013/03/13/174195695/serendipitous-interaction-key-to-tech-firms-workplace-design

CPSIA information can be obtained at www.ICGtesting.com
Printed in the USA
BVOW06s0458290716

457097BV00039B/73/P

The Practice and Philosophy of Decision Making: A Seven Step Spiritual Guide

ISBN: 1-58898-954-2

To order additional copies, please contact us.
BookSurge, LLC
www.booksurge.com
1-866-308-6235
orders@booksurge.com

The Practice and Philosophy of Decision Making: A Seven Step Spiritual Guide

---

Neerja Raman

BOOKSURGE PUBLISHING
2008

Praise for The Practice and Philosophy of Decision Making: A Seven Step Spiritual Guide

"As the world moves faster, it is pioneers like Neerja Raman that lead us towards a stronger understanding of the need for core values and ethics in our everyday life. Professionally successful, Neerja shares her simplistic steps to living in today's global landscape with both its overwhelming opportunities and challenges.

Easy to Comprehend. Simple to Adopt. Powerful to execute. Neerja Raman shows her understanding of how personal and professional spirits collide, compliment and work in conjunction. Balance at business is getting harder and harder but Neerja helps paint a strategy for success inside and outside the workplace.

Daring you to soar to your personal best, Neerja Raman's book provides a distinct path to success. She delivers a plan of action that anyone can start to apply for immediate results. The steps are clear, concise and easy to adopt. Reading the book can be your first step towards a better you."

-*Diana Rohini LaVigne*, www.rohinizone.com

“I was curious about what Neerja had to say that would link decision making today to the ancient Gita but was equally apprehensive about it being merely yet another religious interpretation.

But she pleasantly drew a beautiful line between the deep philosophical undertones of the Gita to self-introspection as the guide to decision making. She reintroduced Dharma as the concept of guidance through personal values, Yoga as the concept of discipline and Gnyana as the concept of self-fulfillment and happiness through Knowledge.

Neerja is a sweet cool breeze for burned realists like me by addressing questions about Reason vs. Emotion, Decisions vs. Strategy and Excellence vs. Perfection. If you want a refreshing non-religious treatise in the art of decision making in life, then get a copy and enjoy!”

-*Supriya Raman*, www.supriyaraman.com

“I enjoyed reading the book, which has a unique language and presentation. The words come from a certain inspiration and conviction, it seems to me.

The book gives a good picture of the teachings of the Geeta to newcomers. Readers will know the range of topics that the ancient poem covered. The highlighted topics can impress young people. Stories with valuable messages like the one on Two Cats and a second on The Happy Man make the reading quite delightful and easy. The section on six kinds of emotional traps and how to handle them, at the end of the book, add value to the work. The Seven Principles are well outlined. The classification of people into child, youth, householder and elder and their description seem to have an original flavor in them. Quotations from Gandhi and Goethe, Swami

Chinmayananda and Pascal have enriched the book.

Congratulations. Hope you will come out with more such useful, practical writing."

-S Chidananda, www.fowai.net

For Papa and Amma

The Practice and Philosophy of Decision Making: A Seven Step Spiritual Guide

TABLE OF CONTENTS

AUTHOR'S NOTE

This book is not about the *Bhagavad Geeta*. It is also not about the workplace or home or the self. My goal is to make the unique philosophy articulated so eloquently in the *Bhagavad Geeta* accessible to today's young adult and to someone like myself—one not literate in Sanskrit and not particularly spiritual and definitely not religious. I also wanted to make it applicable and practical to everyday situations at work or at home. I am fortunate in having spent my childhood years in India where I routinely heard and read about the values espoused in the *Geeta* without knowing the source. Also, though I did not know it at that time, my father was an embodiment of the principles of the *Geeta* so as I have grown older, when life seems too complex and full of conflict, I have a role model. From my mother, I learned the value of literature and the love of books. This helped me manage an apprehension about my ability to experience the *Bhagavad Geeta* through translations in Hindi and English. Overcoming my limitations in this area has given me the courage to interpret the *Geeta* in a more casual and personal way.

I especially wanted to make the *Geeta* accessible to those

who may not want to experience it because they think of it as a religious text or too profound and abstract to be practical. I have tried to keep the translated verses simple. My sources are *Geeta* translations in Hindi and English and discussions with friends and family.

Finally, I acknowledge that I am stymied by the pronoun problem. Awkward and inconsistent use of the masculine and feminine pronoun is meant to indicate equal applicability of the text to all humans.

Acknowledgements

This is not an accurate or scholarly translation of the *Bhagavad Geeta* but more an emotional interpretation of a book I originally read intellectually to understand my "Hinduism." After all, most if not all religions have a book identified to hold the values that govern world order, and the Hindus have not one but several such texts. Only later, in trying to apply it to everyday life did I realize that the *Geeta* must not just be read. It must be experienced and for that I am grateful to many scholars, teachers and philosophers and most of all to my family. This is a personal account of my experiences and hence, I have tried not to litter the whole book with references. However, the insights would not be there for me without the help of many others. The mistakes are mine but I have drawn heavily from ideas of others and I acknowledge them in the bibliography and reference guide. It is an informal listing of the books I have been most influenced by and have either paraphrased or quoted from. Finally, thanks and appreciation is due to my editor for pointing out inconsistent use of language and suggesting clarifications.

Preface

We all make decisions. We make decisions every day.

We make decisions on topics ranging from the mundane (should I eat healthy for lunch today?) to mediocre (should I ask my boss for a raise?) to the momentous (is he my life partner?). No matter what the situation and what our role- leader or follower, manager or employee, mother or daughter- decision making is the process of converting an insight into action, into life. As human beings we are hardwired to choose correctly when it comes to making a life threatening decision, such as fight or flight in times of danger. However, in today's globally connected and interdependent landscape, decisions are less likely to be about survival and more about quality of life. Yet we often make choices based on built in biases that optimize short term results over life-long consequences. This book is about creating a long lasting and individual framework for making choices for the self in the context of community and society based on personal values, the situation at hand and evolving from a compassionate win-win mindset rather than the short term hardwired win-lose view required for survival in the wild.

Assimilation of the ancient wisdom of the Bhagavad Geeta with practical lessons from today's environment provides a novel and contemporary approach to the process of decision-making, consensus building, conflict resolution and self-empowerment. My approach will be to show how we can realize greater fulfillment in our everyday lives by embracing the timeless principles of self-discipline, pursuit of knowledge and non-attachment.

Decision making is a skill, like long distance running is a skill. I must train my body and my mind, stay healthy, take advantage of my natural abilities while managing my limitations, understand the terrain (or context) and practice, practice, practice. Knowing that I have done my best I can relax and excel in action. The rest is up to God.

INTRODUCTION

In eighteen chapters, seven hundred verses, the *Bhagavad Geeta* devotes itself to one task—making one decision. It does so through its protagonist, the warrior Arjun, and the metaphor of war. It does so by enabling Arjun to undertake a voyage of self-discovery so he can master the art of making a complex decision in the face of conflicting values.

In this time of galloping change and global families, people are seeking new ideals and new paradigms. Paradoxically, it can be enlightening to look back at ancient philosophies that have endured historically, ones that have withstood the test of time. As traditional definitions of success and power crumble and technology overtakes our biorhythms, the need for decisive action becomes greater than ever. Texts like the *Bhagavad Geeta* can be a source of knowledge and guidance. This is important today, more than ever, when we have far more options than we did before, because decision making is about making a choice; about taking charge of our life; about feeling in control of our own destiny; about self-empowerment.

Why do we need a philosophical approach to decision making?

A decision is a choice. As soon as you choose to do one thing, it means you are not doing another. That other may have its own advocates of logic, emotion and people. This means dealing with conflict. You will need to stand firm in your choice in the face of opposition from people and circumstance. Having a philosophy will help you understand yourself and your own motives for making the choice in the first place. This in turn will provide you the strength and endurance during this opposition. At the very least, you too will not turn against yourself and if you choose to do so, you will know why. William Ralph Inge is supposed to have said, "The object of studying philosophy is to know one's own mind, not other people."

However, thinking about decisions from a perspective of conflict resolution is going about it the wrong way. Conflict resolution is like happiness; the more you chase it the less likely you are to get it. Just as you cannot get happiness by seeking it you cannot resolve a conflict as long as you see it as a conflict because you will be thinking in terms of winners and losers, us and them. You will need to enlarge your thoughts to a domain large enough to see the problem as a solution rather than as a conflict.

In *The Practice and Philosophy of Decision Making*, I describe an action oriented decision framework, enhanced by philosophical concepts of discipline (*yoga*) and the pursuit of knowledge (*jnana*), uniquely integrating the softer skills of human psychology and philosophy with the traditional hard skills such as planning and action.

"The teaching of the *Geeta* must be regarded not merely in the light of a general spiritual philosophy or ethical doctrine, but as bearing upon a practical crisis in the application of ethics and spirituality to human life." —Sri Aurobindo

PART I

Bhagavad Geeta

The story, context, dilemma and the controversy

The *Bhagavad Geeta* is a poem of 700 verses divided into 18 lessons written in Sanskrit. It is a self contained chapter and an episode in the great epic poem *Mahabharata* which is one hundred thousand verses, eight times longer than the Iliad and Odyssey combined.

Sanskrit is a very compact language and much can be expressed in a few sentences. Combine that with the subject matter of the poem, and the *Geeta* has as many interpretations possible as there are individuals. This is the enduring allure and challenge of the *Geeta* and interestingly a concrete embodiment of its central theme; that we are one in our diversity and individuality. A literal translation of the title would be "Song of the lord" but this is misleading as the *Geeta* is a psychological, philosophical, spiritual poem composed in the form of a dialogue between the warrior Arjuna and his charioteer, the god Krishna. The term philosophy is a compound of two words: *philo* and *sophia,* which mean "love for knowledge." The *Geeta* is that and much more in that it is rooted in the psychology of human beings, represented by Arjuna, thus making it very practical and pragmatic. And yet it goes even further by having a spiritual element expressed in the exhortations of Krishna to Arjuna as he helps him understand and transcend the conflicts encountered in daily life, duty and action. Thus it engages the human intellect, spirit, body and heart. In Sanskrit, the poem would be called "Brahma Vidya." That term conveys an approach to knowledge that leads to knowledge of the Self of all or *Brahman.*

Although the *Geeta* exists as a separate independent poem, it has been placed as an episode in the *Mahabharata* to give it a concrete context while providing an enduring metaphor. As you read the *Geeta*, you realize that the author regularly refers back to the battle as the metaphor. It becomes clear that the author never intended for this to be an abstract document for the learned few but a pragmatic voice to exhort all of us to be the best we can be. Every philosophical reference is followed by concrete advice followed by a supportive text showing understanding of the human struggle.

The Story of *Mahabharata:*

Dhritrashtra is the eldest son of the royal family of Kurukshetra. He has been born blind and hence cannot be crowned king. His younger brother Pandu assumes the throne and Dhritrashtra continues to live in the palace as his advisor. Dhritrashtra is reconciled to this situation but it is a constant struggle for him not to let his feelings of jealousy and injustice take over his actions. As time passes, Dhritrashtra has a hundred sons called the Kauravas and Pandu has five sons called Pandavas. Pandu dies at an early age and so the Pandavas are placed in the care of their uncle Dhritrashtra, who acts as the regent king till the eldest Pandava son, Yudhishtir, comes of age. All the Kauravas and the Pandavas are taught by the same teachers, are schooled in the martial arts and grow up together. All the brothers become excellent in the art of war, but the sons of Pandu have many outstanding qualities of compassion and justice while the Kauravas exhibit a jealous and selfish attitude. When it comes time for the eldest Pandava, Yudhishtir, to become king, the eldest Kaurava whose name is Duryodhan is not satisfied with the situation. He covets the throne so he devises several plots to kill Yudhishtir and his brothers. These plots fail. Then he devises other ways to take away Yudhishtir's right to the throne. He sets up a crooked game of dice and challenges the Pandavas to play. The Pandavas lose the game of dice and their penalty is thirteen years in exile. During this time, the Pandava brothers encounter many hardships and challenges, which they overcome, to emerge stronger and wiser while Duryodhan continues in his unjust ways. When they return to reclaim the kingdom, Duryodhan refuses to step aside. He does not even give them a place to stay anywhere in the kingdom and war becomes inevitable. As the two sides begin gathering armies, both leaders decide to go to Sri Krishna, who has the most powerful army of all, and is also the acknowledged center of wisdom to ask for help. Sri Krishna decides he must be impartial to all so he offers to help one side with his vast army and to the other, he offers himself as a charioteer and counselor. The Kauravas quickly choose the army and the Pandavas choose to have Sri Krishna. A detailed description of the eighteen days of war that follow, and the philosophy of the various gurus and teachers occupy the rest of the *Mahabharata*.

The war ends with the Pandavas victorious—a triumph of good over evil, order over chaos, justice over lawlessness. It is a symbol of the victory of the positive forces over the negative ones functioning within the human heart and mind as well as in the universe. There is a constant battle going on within each individual to regain the lost kingdom of peace, happiness and harmony. The Kauravas represent the negative forces within oneself that must be overcome to achieve that goal. The Pandavas represent the good that is in all of us that must triumph if we are to find harmony on this earth and in this cycle of birth and death.

The Context for the *Geeta*

The setting of the *Bhagavad Geeta* is the battlefield of Kurukshetra on the eve of war. The scene is set with the two armies facing one another in battle formation. Arjuna, the second Pandu son is the leader of the Pandavas army and his charioteer is Sri Krishna. Old King Dhritrashtra, who is blind, stands on a hill overlooking the battlefield and asks his charioteer Sanjaya, to tell him what is happening on the field of battle. Sanjaya has been given the third eye of visionaries, so that when he thinks with his mind, he will see everything taking place during the day or night, in public or in secret. Sanjaya is a metaphor for the third eye that exists in all of us and has the power to "see." Thus, in the *Bhagavad Geeta* or "The Song of the Lord," the mystery of life and death as revealed to Arjuna by Krishna is preserved for all to hear through the mediating voice of Sanjaya and through our third eye.

The battle scene is symbolic of the inner conflict in man. Kurukshetra is not only a physical place but is representative of the state of mind. The opening verse spoken by Dhritrashtra sets the stage for the entire text of the *Geeta,* concisely stating this universal conflict. He demands of Sanjaya: "Tell me what my sons and the sons of Pandu did when they gathered to battle on the field of Kuru, on the field of *Dharma*."

The word *Dharma* in Sanskrit means a combination of sacred duty, law, justice, righteousness and religion. Once the context of war has been set and the metaphor established for good and evil forces warring within oneself, the focus shifts from the action on the field to Arjuna's inner conflict. Arjuna is in an abyss of dejection and despair. He cannot bring himself to act in a ritual of carnage and destruction. Further, he is having a moral struggle on the field of war in doing his duty. He is tormented in having to battle his own kinsmen and his *gurus* and teachers who have made him the great warrior that he is. Understanding what his action should be, is the subject of the *Geeta*. Krishna is the philosopher, psychologist, friend and spiritual counselor, who pours his dialogue into Arjuna's tortured soul to help Arjuna decide what he must do, why he must do it and how to prepare emotionally and physically so he can do what must be done with the excellence required of him.

Throughout the text of the *Geeta*, Arjuna asks probing questions and expresses his dissatisfaction with the apparent inconsistencies in Krishna's answers. This is a critical element of the *Geeta*. Arjuna's voice serves in providing a voice to the reader's own doubts and questions, making it easier to internalize and retain the message that is being given. Even more importantly, it serves to illustrate that only the open and questioning mind can be exposed to advanced and higher thinking. Thus, in a very pragmatic way, we are constantly encouraged to be in a state of a constant seeking of knowledge of the self and God as the path to salvation. It also means one should always follow the dictates of one's conscience. We must believe in what we do; otherwise we will do it half-heartedly. When a human being considers doing something, his conscience helps him choose what he will do by placing the consequences of his actions—good or bad, helpful or damaging, right or wrong—in front of him. By following his conscience, he will choose the correct action and he will have a firm will. Then he will be able to carry out the action he chooses in the very best way possible. *Sankalpa shakti* (will power) is the inner power and is the most powerful force in a human being.

The Decision and Arjuna's Dilemma

In the beginning, Arjuna feels he is motivated to engage in war for the rewards of victory: power and wealth. This he feels is lowly and not worth the inevitable carnage and destruction of war. He cannot destroy his own kinsmen, ruin their families and bring about chaos. He feels pity for his kinsmen and feels he is being unfaithful to his teachers. He is prepared to lay down his arms and not go into battle. But what is his duty? He is a trained warrior, the leader of the army, a revered hero and the prime hope of the Pandava army. What is his duty towards those who bravely go into battle with him? Does the battle signify the triumph of good forces in the Pandavas over the evil and unjust ways of the Kauravas? So what should he do? This is what he inquires of Krishna as he asks him to halt the chariot so he can observe both armies lined up facing each other on the eve of battle.

Krishna observes that Arjuna is driven to fight by the egoism of strength; he is turned from battle by the contrary egoism of pity and disgust. Compassion for mankind will bring clarity of knowledge. The decision criterion is within him. He must free his soul from craving and attachment to inaction as well as action, attachment to various forms of virtue as well as the attractions of sin. To do this he must see the Whole Truth; behold the Self that is a part of the Whole just as the Whole is embodied in the Self. To do that is to get rid of "I" and "my" forms of thinking; to reject the egoism of refusing to work through the universal being as well as the egoism of serving the individual mind and body to the exclusion of others. When he expands his thinking to comprehend reality beyond the physical body, his and others', he will see that the soul is indestructible. In verse II:27 of *Geeta*:

> "Certain is death for the born and certain is birth
> for the dead; therefore what is inevitable should
> not be a cause for grief."

Thus, rather than thinking of war in terms of death and destruction, contemplate the inevitability of the rising and setting sun. They both serve a purpose.

And Krishna says (II:37):

> "If you are killed, you attain heaven,

> If you triumph, you enjoy the earth,
> Therefore, Arjuna, arise, resolved upon battle."

If we were to stop here, this may seem an oversimplification and hence unsatisfying. Even if intellectually this makes sense, the heart rebels. The other lesson here is that no one else can make a decision for you; so Krishna gives his advice in the beginning but after the dialogue asks Arjuna to make his own decision. So the remaining sixteen lessons address the alignment of the intellect, body and heart and what follows is the real teaching of the *Geeta*; the practice of non-attachment as expressed in verse II:38

> "Make grief and happiness, gain and loss, victory and defeat, immaterial to your soul, and turn to battle."

It is a classic illustration of the pragmatic nature of the *Geeta* that a choice must be made in the face of apparent conflict. For each person this choice may be different, but it must be well considered and based upon their circumstance, their training and their duty. My interpretation of the message given here is that whatever the choice or action is determined to be, one must excel at it. And excellence can only be achieved through a state of non-attachment for attachment clouds judgment (II:48) and dilutes will power as we hope for positive outcomes instead of focusing on the task at hand.

Bringing the concept to an even more practical level, thinking about results causes us to worry. Energy that could be utilized in improving execution is spent worrying. Worrying about the results is wasted energy. *Geeta* advises us to:

> "Be intent on action, not on the fruits of action;
> as well as attachment to inaction."

This is another good example of the power of combining philosophy and human psychology. Non-attachment is a goal and a powerful tool in allowing us to maintain humility in a success and confidence after a failure. We know it is distracting and a waste of energy to worry about the future probabilities so it is best not to dwell on consequences. By practicing non-attachment to results while in the midst of action, we can be more effective. This point is possibly the single-most misinterpreted part of the *Geeta*. Non-attachment is practiced so that we will be more effective at what we choose to do, not because fate will deliver whatever results it may and we need do nothing.

A key enabler in performing well is discipline. The Sanskrit word *Yoga* has probably even more meanings than the word *Dharma*. A healthy body and a steadfast mind are the goals of yogic exercises. Preparation, good judgment, self-confidence and a stable intelligence are required for excellent execution.

> "Perform actions, firm in *yoga* (discipline),
> relinquishing attachment;
> be impartial to failure and success-
> this equanimity is called *yoga*."

Intelligence can be clouded by delusions and can be fleeting, meaning that it can lead us in different directions, resulting in a lack of focus. Once again there is the emphasis on non-attachment. It will be a steadying influence because love and hatred, grief and happiness, failure and success, friends and foes all can equally mar judgment.

Krishna also goes on to explain what discipline looks like. First he says, "discipline is skill in actions" and then goes on to elaborate (II:53):

> "When your understanding turns from sacred
> lore to stand fixed, immovable in contemplation,
> then you will reach discipline."

In its pragmatic way, the *Geeta* puts our thoughts into the words of Arjuna who asks what this kind of person of understanding looks like? How does he speak, act, sit and move? Krishna says:

> "When he gives up desires in his mind,
> is content with the self within himself,
> then he is said to be a man
> whose insight is sure, Arjuna."

Krishna goes on to elaborate that such a man is free from sorrow, fear and anger. He neither exults nor hates, has no preference for fortune or misfortune, and his cravings for pleasures and attractions have vanished.

> "When, like a tortoise retracting
> its limbs, he withdraws his senses
> completely from sensuous objects,
> his insight is sure."

Thus we learn that personal harmony is both a requirement for excellence as well as a characteristic of one who excels.

While maintaining this emphasis on action, Krishna warns Arjuna to be wary of pride creeping in from his attachment to action itself; even that is weakening. So he says (IV:20):

> "Abandoning attachment to fruits
> of action, always content, independent,
> he does nothing at all
> even when he engages in action."

Once again, my interpretation of this philosophy has a pragmatic value in keeping Arjuna free from getting drawn into the pride of action itself. This is useful later, in keeping him from feeling guilt or arrogance from the results of the action. In this context, guilt arises from having killed his kinsmen in battle, and arrogance comes from the power of winning the battle.

Krishna understands that this is still very difficult for Arjuna to internalize, so he offers the next piece of wisdom. He says humans are instruments of a higher being. God drives their actions. Arjuna can choose to believe in this higher power and consider himself an instrument of God, doing His will. This way, he can free himself from the conflict that is apparent to him. The wise person sees that he is not the doer, but all material acts are the act of Nature (*Prakriti*). The soul (*Atman*) remains a witness. One who understands this will realize the Self—understanding that there is no beginning or end. If an action is done with this kind of devotion, it is not tainted by its results. Just as the single sun illuminates the entire world, so does a person who understands himself understand the Whole.

Towards the end of his discourse, Krishna goes full circle and reinforces the concepts of timelessness and wholeness. He explains: think of the absolute as fullness or infinite. When you add or subtract from the infinite, it is neither increased nor decreased, yet it absorbs what is added and allows whatever needs to leave to leave. Thus the Self is not contained in the three elements or *gunas* of *sattava*, *rajas* and *tamas*. It is above them. The human body performs actions, but the Self remains above them, untainted by their stains and impurities.

The Controversy about War

The opening verses of the *Geeta* establish the context of war. Soon thereafter, Krishna urges Arjuna to do battle against his kinsmen. This fact causes utter confusion in the mind of the reader. The pacifist in us is up in arms, metaphorically speaking, against a philosophy that appears on the surface so cavalier. But is that correct? Does the *Geeta* uphold violence?

It does not. War is a concept humans can understand and exemplifies that no decision is simple. Nature or *Prakriti* is complex. What the *Bhagavad Geeta* upholds is the concept of *dharma*: truth, duty and knowledge. That becomes abundantly clear as you read the remaining verses. The power of the text lies in not making a mystery of what Arjuna's choice is in the context of his birth, his abilities and his position. The *Geeta* outlines a process for making decisions using Arjuna, a prince with a job to do in the context of war as an example.

What is your choice? That is determined by your context. The power lies in the bulk of the verses of the *Geeta* being devoted to urging you and preparing you for making tough choices. The power lies in the integration of psychology, spirituality and just plain pragmatism exhibited in practical health tips and social duties outlined throughout the book.

There is no attempt at smoothing the rough edges of nature, and there are no pat definitions of good and evil. The war is not fought between Gods and Demons representing good and evil. There is no release in the book from constant internal struggle. That is also why there is no linear thread of logic to follow. The verses weave practical and philosophical strands because that is how the human intellect and heart function. This makes for difficult reading for some but easier internalization for those who actually are facing a difficult decision and read the *Geeta* for realizing their inner strength.

Mahatma Gandhi, whose name is synonymous with non-violence, who believed in the unity of mankind, who drew no distinctions between religions, races and countries was greatly influenced by the *Geeta*. I admit that I do find great support and solace in that. To me he embodied the ability to resolve apparent conflicts by seeing the Whole in the context of truth and knowledge. He said his actions were devoted to the welfare of all. Of nonviolence he said, "the dignity of man requires obedience to a higher law—the strength of the spirit." He, like Arjuna, fought for freedom with action.

For Gandhi action was the weapon of non-violence. Isn't that what the *Geeta* says? That in the ultimate, who can say what is action, what is inaction?

At the Harijan march of 1936, Gandhi said:

> "I have nothing new to teach the world. Truth and nonviolence are as old as the hills."

The *Geeta* makes sure that in espousing this higher philosophy, one does not get confused between what is right and what is wrong. It maintains a forgiving attitude towards those whose motives are pure even if their actions are not and says that the learned sage sees no hierarchy between God's creatures. All have an equal chance at gaining nirvana. But Krishna also enunciates *Prakriti* (nature) and the three *Gunas* (attributes) to acknowledge the internal struggle of all humans.

The universe is made manifest through three attributes or elements. Anyone who has a body has the attributes that bind the soul, keep it earthbound, and prevent it from attaining nirvana. By elucidating the attributes, Krishna takes away any feelings of guilt that may be induced by the struggle against our own baser instincts. He says, it is OK, it is natural and even acknowledges that it is a struggle in which you will not always be the victor. That too is OK as long as you try your best. Guilt is another emotion (like worry) which is a waste of energy and Krishna finds no value in it.

According to the *Geeta* there are three elements that make up the universe:

Truth or lucidity (*sattva*) is the highest, it is the illuminator and healthy and it binds the soul to this universe through the attraction to knowledge. Note that this is a passive state and in the context of war, nonviolence is a passive state and a higher means to the same goal.

Passion (*rajas*) is next and binds through attachment to action. Cravings and emotions characterize it and so it sees great conflict as a consequence. Note that it is an active state, and violence in the context of war is a means that generates great conflict within us.

Dark inertia (*tamas*) is born of ignorance and it binds through sloth and negligence. It is the stupefier of all body owners. There is really no easy way to describe this state other than as an opposite of true knowledge.

Truth causes attachment to happiness, passion to action, but the lowest is dark inertia because it veils knowledge and causes attachment to negligence or laziness.

All objects in this universe are manifestations by nature of a combination of the three elements. Transcending these three elements, which make up the body allows one to escape the cycle of birth. For those born on this earth, says Krishna (XIV:6):

> "Lucidity (sattva), being immaculate,
> is illuminating and flawless;
> it binds through self-identification
> with happiness and wisdom.
>
> Know that passion (rajas) is emotional,
> being born of cupidity and craving;
> it binds the soul through attachment
> to actions and their fruits.
>
> And know dark inertia (tamas),
> The deluder of all embodied beings,
> As born of ignorance;
> It binds one with indolence, sloth and sleep.
>
> Arjuna, sattva urges one to happiness
> And rajas to action,
> While tamas, clouding wisdom,
> Urges one to negligence."

Krishna embellishes the concepts with details of how these three elements are distinct yet are ever present and act in coordination. The vigilant aspirant is ever watchful of keeping inertia and passion tamed and contained so that with the help of lucidity, he may ascend the path to salvation, undisturbed and undistracted. Krishna advises the aspirant to practice meditation and seek strength from the inner soul since that is the source of the greatest power.

When *sattva* is predominant the aspirant remains serene, calm and happy and elevating thoughts dawn during this time. This element is full of delight and enlightenment and is helpful in maintaining mental and emotional equilibrium. When this quality is not predominant one experiences a lack of calmness leading to inner turmoil and conflict.

Examples of domination of *rajas* are feelings of pain and pleasure, attachment and hatred. A person who is dominated by these emotions is never satisfied, constantly pursuing objects of pleasure. Such a person is prone to disease because he does not have the discipline to control his appetites and practice moderation. Often such a person acts on unconscious habits and impulses, not understanding why he does what he does. Thus criminals may confess knowing that they have done wrong, but could not help doing what they did. This element can be directed positively and can be an active force if properly utilized both for the individual and for mankind. This can be done by consciously utilizing the knowledge one has to fight through the conflict one sees and pursue action.

Tamas is sloth and inertia; it produces ignorance causing negligence and destroys the sense of discrimination. It creates delusions and then one cannot make decisions. This leads one to inaction and further, a feeling of being justified in their inaction. A lazy aspirant remains in a state of lethargy and experiences negative feelings resulting in withdrawal from society. He or she is controlled by negative emotions and is prone to mental disorders as well as physical diseases brought upon by inertia.

These three elements dwell in every body, and different ones may be predominant based on circumstance. There is great wisdom in recognizing these elements as being universal. It enables one to focus on improving oneself and not being judgmental of others. When we recognize others practicing in a lower state we can just see in them ourselves as in a mirror. We know we are the same as the other and we can then be helpful and compassionate rather than judgmental and vindictive. Just as we do not hurt our own body, even if it is diseased or handicapped, likewise we do not hurt others as they are a mirror of ourselves.

When we extend the metaphor of our own body, a whole that consists of many parts, none of which we willingly hurt, to all of mankind and the universe, a clearer picture emerges. We must fight and overcome internal and external forces that keep us from seeking Truth and knowledge. Extend the metaphor to war and there is guidance on what the warrior's action must be. By placing his actions in the context of the elements that make up the universe, Arjuna can make peace with his act of war.

PART II

Dharma, Yoga, Jnana

The three pillars of individual strength

Dharma—The concept of guidance through values

"Behavior is a mirror in which every one displays his own image"—Goethe

What is *Dharma?*

Essentially untranslatable, the word *dharma* is derived from the root word *dhri* meaning to hold or sustain. A man's *dharma* is the basis of his thought and action. *Dharma* is what defines a person, giving him strength to be who he is, his character, his attitude, his inner core. *Svadharma*, individual and personal *dharma* of a man, is determined by his past experiences, including experiences in past lives which are stored up in the soul and not destroyed upon the death of a body. These experiences make up one's *svabhava* or character and how he or she will act. They determine an individual's duty, religion, philosophy, beliefs, inclinations, instincts, nature, and his or her *dharma*.

"He who does the duty ordained by his own nature incurs no sin." Thus in the eyes of God we are all equal and our actions are appropriate to our nature. The natural *dharma* of one is not the same as that of another. The duty of a soldier is to fight while the duty of a teacher is to teach. What is right for one is not the right action for the other. Thus, Krishna asks Arjuna to find the answer to his dilemma, the decision to fight or not, by listening to the voice of his inner core, his *dharma*, his upbringing, his duty. His natural duty is the only reality for him; all others, the duties or viewpoints of others are distractions, imposed from the outside and thus confusing. "One should not abandon one's innate duty imperfect as it may appear to be; for all worldly enterprises are imperfect, like fire is rendered imperfect by smoke."

While untranslatable, the meaning of *dharma* is abundantly clear when used in context. Instinctively, we understand the concept and can act on it. Once we accept that our decisions and actions are driven by our *dharma*, not our ego, it becomes possible to act with humility, with non-attachment, without judgment of our fellow beings, without pride in the results of doing good, or sorrow in the results of doing evil. We understand that the universe is made up of opposites, good and evil, pain and pleasure, life and death. A perfect world containing goodness or happiness only is a contradiction in terms; creation is possible only in a state of chaos, of dissolution. If everybody were perfect, the world would cease to exist. Thus, acceptance of the contradictions that constitute Nature reduces inner conflict. We learn to draw strength from within and focus on being an instrument of God or another power higher than we are.

Why *Dharma?* For Self-Empowerment

The study of Ethics concerns itself with the sorts of actions that constitute virtuous conduct. What kinds of actions ought to be undertaken? What is right? What is wrong? What is good? What is bad? However, the problem with this approach is that the absolute guidance it seeks does not exist. Soon we build a complex set of assumptions that fail to satisfy us in all circumstances and we are back to square one. With this approach, the apparent contradictions that make up Nature cannot be resolved. A logical disenchantment leads to emotional frailty and a lack of a feeling of being in control of our own destiny.

To the question "What should I do?" the *Bhagavad Geeta* says, "Do your righteous duty; be guided by your *Dharma*." The intellectual appeal of the *Geeta* is that it never proposes an edict that one could disagree with. Emotionally, it is equally powerful in forcing us to believe in an overall goodness and a sense of justice that must exist even if we cannot perceive it in our lifetime. There is no concept of evil or sin. Every contradiction can be resolved if you believe that the space, time, environment axes are greater than what we perceive in our individual lifetime. Logically we know that to be true anyway. Empires crumble and are born again. Families prosper and lose their wealth. Intelligence is found in all corners of humanity. What is good for you can hurt me. A lion must hunt the deer. Nature has a rhythm all its own. Justice eventually prevails if you believe that every action is a will of God.

Thus, there is no absolute definition of right or wrong, good or bad for a person. Deal with right and wrong in the context of the individual in a society, environment and time. There is no good or bad in an absolute sense for a person born to this earth because an individual can only relate to the space, time and environment that he or she is born into. There is good and bad in an absolute sense and only someone, God, who can see across infinite time, space and planets can judge right or wrong in the absolute. This precludes anyone born to this earth. This precludes you and me from having any right to be judgmental of another's actions. If they have done wrong, they will be punished in ways we may not see. Only God has the power to judge actions. This point cannot be overemphasized, as it is the core belief in making your *dharma* a "good" *dharma*. In this premise, everybody's *dharma* becomes a good *dharma*—essentially a circular logic, central to the theme of the *Geeta*, works because of this faith.

Be guided by your *dharma*, and you can do no wrong in the eyes of God. Whatever you do, that is the right thing to do as long as you have listened to your heart, your inner voice. I can't think of a better way to empower yourself.

> "Sages see with an equal eye the learned and cultured Brahmin, the cow, the elephant, the dog"

Why *Dharma*? Excellence in Action

When doing good, it is easy to fall into the trap of feeling virtuous. This is just as dangerous as feeling remorse when doing something bad. Therefore, it is best not to see yourself as doing good or bad. Such thinking leads us to see conflict and reduces our inner strength. Krishna's dialogue with Arjuna is lengthy because he will not allow Arjuna to believe he must engage in the battle of Kurukshtra because it is a war of good over evil. Arjuna must engage in battle because this is his *dharma*; his *dharma* being determined by his birth as a prince; his education as a warrior; his position as the leader of his army; his talent for archery that made him the superb fighter that he is, etc. In short, his birth, the makeup of his experiences and his character—his *dharma*—determines his actions. He may see himself as an instrument of God in fighting the battle. That will give him strength and inner conviction but he is not allowed to believe that he can be the one to decide he is waging a war of good over evil. If you think about it, you will see that there is great logic in this.

The context of the *Mahabharata* clearly sets the stage for the evil ways of the kauravas. Krishna even acknowledges that with his divine sight, he sees that a battle must be fought to restore the balance in this world. But Arjuna is not allowed to use this crutch, this feeling of righteousness. For a crutch it is and not a very lasting one. War means killing your loved ones. How can there be any sustained feeling of doing good in a situation like that? The realities of battle are harsh and a crutch like that will not withstand the devastation that is a natural outcome of war. Perception of conflict creates inner turmoil. It will weaken Arjuna's ability to act as he must, as the unerring marksman that he is, trained to be so by his revered teacher, who is to be his mark.

Why *Dharma?* Self-fulfillment

Krishna teaches us that fulfillment lies in the action itself, not in the result of actions. Action dictated by our *dharma* is our salvation irrespective of the result. Self-fulfillment comes from knowing we have done what we must do—executed the will of God. Do your best and all will be well. If we get caught up with results, it means we feel pride in doing good, guilt in doing harm. Who is to know if what is good today will still be considered good tomorrow?

Action and execution of actions with excellence is what you control. Drawing satisfaction from that is essential. This is a necessary corollary to the thesis that good and bad is not for you to judge. There are no good or bad results, either, if the context is large enough.

When you ask, "What is a pentagon?" there is one answer defined by science. When you ask, "What is sweet?" there is one answer defined by your senses. When you ask, "What is good or what is bad?" there is no absolute definition because we do not have an absolute sense of it and there can be no pervasive definition.

Most people would agree with Hamlet: "There is nothing good or bad, but thinking makes it so." Thus in the context of Ethics, it is impossible to define an absolute answer to "What actions ought people take?" But in the context of an individual in a certain situation at a given time the answer is simple—do your duty. What your duty is should be a way of life for you so every action is not a major decision. Hence it is also called your *dharma*, your guiding principles, your philosophy, and your religion or righteous duty.

Arjuna is a warrior by profession, leader of his army and he is in a battle. His righteous duty is to raise arms in battle. Questioning the merits of war and the destruction of his kith and kin detracts from his ability to engage in action in a superior fashion. If he is to excel in action, he must not act halfheartedly. Thus, Arjuna is never asked by Krishna to believe that killing his brother is good or that he is a better person for killing an evil man. The *Geeta* never says that war is good or violence is condoned. Quite the opposite. Death and destruction are painful consequences of the act of war and given Arjuna's role in it he must detach himself from feeling pride in victory or guilt in loss.

Your duty is not defined by your absolute measure of right or wrong. Who you are, what your circumstances are and right and wrong in that context define how you will operate. If you happen to be a very enlightened individual you may be able to understand why your duty is what it is in the context of society and the time you are in, but that may be difficult and is not required. Sages, *rishis*, and *munis* who meditate at length in desolate mountains in the search of the true self may be able to understand the cosmos, but it is not possible for most humans and not required. Thus, the war of Kurukshetra and the destruction of war is justified by Krishna as inevitable because a higher being, God, has decided it is the right action because of the increasingly evil ways of the Kauravas. But that is not for Arjuna to decide. He is not to feel a sense of superiority over his goodness and engage in a war of good over evil. He is to remain humble in his actions in performing his duty.

Dharma Provides a Structure for Change

A great barrier to decision-making is the fear of change.

After all, choices lead to action and action leads to change. Studies show that even good changes like getting a job, marriage, an inheritane or even winning a lottery cause almost as much stress as unwelcome changes. From birth to death, we go through physical and emotional change, our inner core is constantly undergoing modifications; every life experience changes us and influences our interaction with the environment.

To accept change as the norm and to accept that we ourselves must change as we go through life is built into the concept of *dharma*. Having a structure that sets expectations for different criteria for decision-making and different value systems as we progress from birth to adulthood and old age improves our ability to interact with others who are in different phases of life. It promotes a less judgmental attitude, as it becomes easier to see oneself in the other person's shoes.

Life is divided into four approximate stages, *ashrams*, where one's *dharma*, primary pursuit or duty, criteria for decision-making and framework for action is appropriate to the stage of life one is in. *Brahmacharya* or childhood is the first stage of life when one is molded and prepared to live a good life. In this phase one should be guided by the discipline of learning, seeking knowledge. True knowledge cannot be acquired without cultivating an ability to have complete faith and trust. This mental and emotional development can best be acquired by serving one's teacher, the guru, as a disciple. Princes, such as Arjuna, lived in the forest with teachers such as Dronacharya, in spartan conditions, far from cities where all students, prince or commoner, were taught under similar conditions and it was up to the teacher to decide when they would graduate. Complete allegiance to the teacher was expected of the students, as it was believed that one must learn with the heart, not just the mind.

The second stage, *grahastha ashram*, is when one becomes a contributing member of society. Typically, this stage is marked by sensory and aesthetic fulfillment; material and social ambitions are realized as a householder and by having a position, a job, work where one can apply the knowledge gained during childhood. Arjuna is in this stage when the battle of Kurukshetra takes place. He is a prince and a soldier, and when he is at war his decision framework is different from when he was a student. This is the argument Krishna uses to reduce the conflict in Arjuna's mind when going into battle against his revered teacher and guru whom he respects more than his own life.

Renunciation must be practiced in the next stage of life in an aspiration to achieve liberation from worldly pursuits. This means giving up control of family affairs while reducing one's physical and emotional needs and practicing detachment from action itself. A very natural development, this phase is an acknowledgement of the fact that as we go through life, we cease to draw satisfaction from the sorts of activities that we enjoyed earlier in life, and so the best course of action is to move on to other things. The journey is more important than the destination, so this phase is the start of a new journey and is preparation, much as childhood was, for the next phase of life.

During the final push for liberation, *moksha,* asceticism can be practiced in the last stage of life by becoming a *sanyasi,* a forest dwelling hermit or a homeless wanderer who answers only to God. It is the duty of a *grahastha* to provide for the physical needs of a homeless wanderer in this stage.

Svadharma, one's own guiding principles for action, one's duty, must be individually defined according to the stage of life and position.

Yoga—The Concept of Discipline

"Discipline is skill in actions"
"Unreal is action without discipline, charity without sympathy, ritual without devotion"
Bhagavad Geeta

What is *Yoga*?

The word *Yoga* has many meanings. *Yoga* is derived from the Sanskrit *Yuj* meaning to bind, join, attach and yoke, to direct and concentrate one's attention on, to use and apply. It has been likened to the Latin word *jungere*, meaning "to join." In the *Light on Yoga,* B.K.S. Iyengar says it also means union or communion. It means "the disciplining of the intellect, the mind, the emotions, the will; it means a poise of the soul which enables one to look at life in all its aspects evenly" says Mahadev Desai in *Geeta According to Gandhi.* "It means the yoking of all the powers of body, mind and soul to God."

One who follows the path of *Yoga* is a *Yogi* (masculine) or *Yogin* (feminine). The goal of a *Yogi* or *Yogin* is to achieve a state that would best be described as the opposite of what psychologists would call alienation or what Buddhists call *sakyadrishti*, the feeling of separateness, of being cut off from being.

In Chapter Six of the *Bhagavad Geeta*, Krishna explains to Arjuna the meaning of *Yoga* as a "deliverance from contact with pain and sorrow."

As a well cut diamond has many facets, each reflecting a different color of light, so does the word *Yoga*, each facet reflecting a different shade of meaning and revealing different aspects of the entire range of human endeavor to win inner peace and happiness.

According to B.K.S. Iyengar, "*Yoga* is a timeless pragmatic science evolved over thousands of years dealing with the physical, moral, mental and spiritual well being of man as a whole." In 200 BC, Patanjali wrote the classic treatise *Yoga Sutras* that systematically expounded on the mental and physical discipline as the path to achieving inner peace. He believed that a person whose mind is free of conflict, free of restlessness is in harmony. Such a person, by the grace of the spirit within him or herself finds fulfillment.

Patanjali describes in detail the physical exercises necessary to hone the instrument that is our body, the environment and conditions such as food and sleep, samadhis or postures to still the mind in preparation for meditation for mental cleansing as well as common obstacles to overcome. It is the foremost and most complete and scientific approach to self-disciple as a path to success, which it defines as personal fulfillment, to be seen in literature.

The practice of *Yoga* requires a firm foundation in self discipline, faith, tenacity and perseverance to practice regularly, without which it could be considered mere acrobatics. According to Iyengar, "To win a battle, a general surveys the terrain and the enemy and plans counter measures. In a similar way the Yogi plans the conquest of the Self."

The Stages of *Yoga*

Patanjali enumerates eight stages or limbs of *Yoga* as the right means in the quest of inner understanding. The eight stages in succession allow one to achieve first, harmony with the environment and other people. Second, they allow the Yogi to control the self—body and mind. Having achieved these two stages a Yogi can then look into the innermost recesses of the body and mind to discover his Soul and his maker who are one and the same.

The first three stages are outward quests, which allow the Yogi to conquer the body and render it a fit vehicle for the Soul. Exercise or *Yama* and a regular routine or *Niyama* control the Yogi's passions and emotions and thus keep him in harmony with his fellow man. Physical postures that increase flexibility of the limbs, regulate our breathing and allow for meditation or *Asanas* keep the body healthy and strong and in harmony with nature.

The next two stages are inner quests and they teach the aspirant to regulate the breathing and thereby control the mind. This helps free the senses from the bonds of desire.

The next three stages are the quest of the Soul. The Yogi knows that there is no need to look heavenward to find God. His inner self is the abode of his maker and this realization keeps him in harmony with himself and his maker.

When one has achieved the ultimate discipline one sees the Whole Truth. In this stage, the knower, the knowledge and the known become one. The seer, the sight and the seen have no separate existence. It is as if a great musician becomes one with the instrument and the music that comes from it. Without one another there is no reality for either of them.

The path of *Yoga* is the foundation for the three different paths to salvation or nirvana or escape from the cycle of birth and death.

Karma Marga is the active person's path. It is the path of action in performing one's duty and doing the work.

Bhakti Marga is the emotional person's path where he or she finds realization through love and devotion to a personal God.

Jnana Marga is the intellectual's path where realization comes from knowledge and from control of his or her mind.

By practicing *Yoga*, the common man can hope to follow the path of Karma Marga, the path of selfless action performed with skill, judgment, goodwill and non-attachment. There is no hierarchy associated with these paths, they are not mutually exclusive and indeed one may follow all three. Ultimately, the three paths merge into one, are the same and are indistinguishable from one another when traveled by an enlightened Yogi.

Distractions on the Path of *Yoga*

Awareness of these distractions and overcoming the obstacles thus encountered are the first indications of self-discipline.

1. Ill health or sickness—a yogi or yogin must keep his or her body in prime condition. Just as an out of tune instrument cannot produce music or a broken vehicle will not travel far, so it is with an injured or unhealthy body. When the body is sick, the mind is restless and meditation is impossible. Practice good diet and exercise.
2. Laziness and indifference—in this condition the mind becomes dull due to inactivity. There is no enthusiasm, there are no goals. Just as flowing water is pure and stagnant water putrid, a listless person is like a living corpse who can do nothing.
3. Faithlessness—self-doubt and ill will characterize this state. Indecision results because of constant doubts and conflicts. Faith is necessary to conquer obstacles and feel happy.
4. Pride—a feeling of self-importance leads to justifying a path that places the needs of oneself above those of

others. This person is afflicted with a false knowledge and lacks the humility to gain wisdom from others.

5. Lack of concentration—In this state one may know what must be done, but cannot summon the stamina to do it. For example, a musician can hear the music in her dream but she cannot play it when she awakens.

Disciplines To Enlist on the Path of *Yoga*

To overcome the obstacles on the path of *Yoga*, practice the following:

1. Friendliness—the discipline of *maitri* or friendship is achieving a feeling of oneness with the object of friendliness; thus, it is much more than friendship. It is a feeling of delight, such as that of a mother in the accomplishments of her child. It is an ability to turn your enemies into your friends by having a feeling of oneness with them.
2. Compassion—much more than pity and much more than action, it is a combination of the two. When you can use all your resources, physical, moral, mental or emotional in the sheltering of the needy and the weak, you show *karuna*. You share your strength with the weak till they can become strong. This is not a "survival of the fittest" discipline.
3. Delight in good work of another—even when the other is your rival or enemy, by showing *mudita*, a Yogin saves herself much heartburn by not being angry or jealous and showing no hatred even when the other achieves a goal which she herself may have failed to achieve.
4. Self-examination—Upon seeing another who may have fallen into vice, *upeksa* is self-examination to understand how one would have behaved when faced with the same temptations. Doing this allows the Yogi to understand the fallen and be charitable towards them while helping him to avoid temptation and stay on the right path.

These are disciplines of the mind and are the hardest to execute. An unquiet mind cannot experience these feelings and act upon them.

Constant Practice and Preparation

Yoga is not a theoretical exercise. Constant practice is the key to being well prepared for action. In fact, *Yoga* places the greatest emphasis on *abhyasa*, or constant practice and calls it a spiritual endeavor. Everyone, young, old, sick and infirm can achieve perfection through dedicated application. Success comes to those who are well prepared. "Seeds must be pressed to yield oil. Wood must be heated to release the fire within. The Yogi must practice to realize his inner potential."

Jnana—The Concept of Harmony through Knowledge

"Action will remove the doubt that theory cannot solve"—Tehyi Hsieh

What is *Jnana*?

The art of self-discovery is the subject of the *Bhagavad Geeta*. Mastering this art may not be possible for all, but to embark on the journey of self-discovery is. Says Krishna, "To know oneself is to know me. To know me is to know that God is the strength in the strong, the intelligence in the intelligent, and the virtue in the righteous, the wisdom in the wise and the heat in the Sun." It is to have the will to engage in action and to understand the embodiment of opposites that reside in body and mind. Self-discovery is the path to true knowledge. True knowledge is self-knowledge. In the context of the *Geeta*, knowledge is a journey as well as a destination. And it is a journey that is full of obstacles. To embark on this journey armed with physical and mental discipline, to live life as a Yogi on this path of true knowledge, no matter what the obstacles, is possible for all and so all can be called knowledgeable. By understanding the obstacles and preparing to overcome them, one who follows the path of true knowledge with faith and devotion has a sense of peace and fulfillment. This is the message of the *Geeta.*

True knowledge cannot be bought or acquired since it comes from within. It comes with experience. It comes from action. Education can be imparted, but knowledge has to be discovered or revealed. Attending language classes can make us proficient in grammar and vocabulary, but cannot make us poets. That ability comes from within. Knowledge is a synthesis of who we are and the world around us. Education provides a partial view, but knowledge allows us to see the whole. Thus education is a tool to be utilized on the journey of knowledge, but education by itself does not guide us onto the right path.

Knowledge gives insight and wisdom and will free us from misconceptions, eliminate false behaviors and actuate a withdrawal from wrong ways of living. This, in turn, generates a feeling of peace and fulfillment with oneself and with the world we live in, a sense of harmony.

In Sanskrit, this knowledge is called *jnana.*

In describing a knowledgeable person, Swami Nikhilananda's translation says: "As the flying bird leaves no footprint in the air and the swimming fish no track in the water, so also the knower of Truth leaves no track or footprint on earth. He is known only to himself and to those who have attained self-knowledge." Even when engaged in the most intense action the true self is immersed in peace and blessedness, and it is only the organs and the senses that busy themselves in this world.

True Knowledge: Sattvic Jnana

The *Bhagavad Geeta* calls true knowledge, the highest form of knowledge, *Sattvic Jnana.* It is the ability to see that which is whole; which is more than the sum of its parts. We see that the "one reality that pervades all differences," "the recognition of oneness in manyness" is the highest knowledge. Our body is a good example of this. When we study anatomy, we see that there are many different parts: heart, lungs, stomach, fingers, toes and head. But I understand that while these are many parts, the whole is I. I understand the oneness that is me. I, as one entity, am pervading all the many parts. The highest knowledge then is to be able to see the one Reality that pervades through all the names and forms of the universe. If you touch my back, I might say, "Why are you touching me?" I, as the one entity, am pervading all the many parts. The importance of having this vision of oneness is that it affects our outlook and how we perceive life, others, and ourselves—how we act and what decisions we make.

How does *Sattvic Jnana* influence behavior?

The most concrete example of true knowledge is our attitude towards our physical body. Suppose I poke myself in the eye while I am talking. I will use the same finger to rub my eye and console it. I will not cut off the finger and throw it away because it has hurt my eye. Sometimes, if I am eating and start talking, my teeth will bite my tongue. Do I break my teeth in order to punish them? No, I do not. My teeth are a part of me and I can no more give them pain than I can my tongue. I have no hatred towards my teeth. So we see that when we have a sense of oneness, we are immediately raised to a higher level of understanding. I have an understanding that involves the individual parts and also the interrelationships. All parts of my physical body are important and I am impartial in my actions to all. I have an attitude of service to all. I have no judgmental reaction. I have no desire to hurt or destroy. My only reaction is to serve and assist.

There is a powerful corollary to this definition of knowledge. If true knowledge, our ability to see the whole, this vision of oneness, brings in us a desire to serve, assist and help, then the moment when we are unable to serve, it means we need to revive our vision. It is not a lack of love or the desire to do well. That is inherent in the nature of our soul and only its manifestation is aberrant. That means you can do something about it and pretty quickly too because all you have to do is change your attitude. The ability is already there; you just have to let it become apparent.

This is an empowering concept. We are born with the ability to serve and assist and to find peace and self-fulfillment. The *Geeta* says that true knowledge is available to us all. We only have to seek it. Just as we know it for our bodies, we can know it for the universe.

If one person finds enlightenment and changes, the world around him will be changed. Each of us influences a great many people. The wise man hates none and is friend to all. Do not wait for others to change; begin with yourself. You are the world and the world is not different from you. This is also called the non-dualism of vedantic knowledge and is the most complete form of knowledge.

Knowledge Traps

Sattvic Jnana is the truest form of knowledge. We can aspire towards *Sattvic Jnana* by recognizing and rising above lower or incomplete forms of knowledge. Those are called *Rajasic Jnana* and *Tamasic Jnana* which are the lowest forms of knowledge. Getting stuck in one of these and perceiving them as the whole is a trap we must avoid.

Rajasic knowledge is the understanding of the parts. This is when one sees each thing separately and as unrelated. We understand the parts but not the whole. An eye specialist may treat the eye, a painter may notice color and form, and a musician may understand the notes. The trap in this is not only in missing the higher experience such as music created from the notes, but in starting to believe that the parts are all important—the notes are more important than the music—that one cannot have music without the notes. This is wrong.

Music comes from within and can be expressed and shared using musical notes, but that is just one method. Music will find expression but probably not from the person who is lost in the notes. This form of partial knowledge is called *Rajasic Jnana* and can be a trap if not recognized.

The lowest form of knowledge is called *Tamasic Jnana* and is a bigger trap. This is when one takes the understanding of a certain part of the whole, and becomes attached to it instead of the whole. This is when I get attached to my view, my object and my path. Then my path becomes the right path. My way is the correct way. The person with *Tamasic* knowledge is intolerant and fanatical. This narrow view of thinking makes everything appear to be a conflict. One sees only winners and losers, only right and wrong, only my way and your way. In seeing things this way there can be no benefit to anyone.

True Knowledge: The Field and the Knower of the Field

Chapter Thirteen of the *Bhagavad Geeta* uses the metaphor of a field (*kshetra*) for the human body and mind and defines true knowledge as the ability to "know" the field. Thus a knowledgeable person is one who "knows" the "field" and is called "knower" of the field (*kshetrajna*). It defines God, in the form of Krishna, to be the "knower" of the field in all "fields," thus having the knowledge of matter and spirit—*Prakriti* and *Purusha*. For Krishna all the fields together are one field. What Arjuna can do is to completely know himself and thus find God within him and thus know matter and spirit.

Self-knowledge is true knowledge and the objective for staying on the path of true knowledge is to find God. Thus devotion to God is the same as devotion to knowledge and is the stabilizing force in a yogi.

What am I? Who am I?

The field, *kshetra*, has been described by sages in many

different ways, says Krishna. Briefly, the field is made up of the five subtle elements (ether, air, fire, water, earth), the ego, the intellect, the faculties of knowing and doing, the five objects of sense (sound, touch, color, taste and smell). Within this field reside the opposites of desire and aversion, pleasure and pain. It embodies consciousness and resolution. The field is constantly evolving, imperfect and subject to change.

While the word "field" is used in almost all English translations of the *Bhagavad Geeta* for the word *kshetra*, I have had some trouble with using this word. Yet, I cannot think of a better word. Suffice it for me that the word "field" itself can have a multiplicity of meanings depending on the context. In the world of physics, field is an abstraction to express a force of nature. Thus, we have an electromagnetic field. It is a force of completely abstract form and shape and can appear or disappear if the conditions are not there to make this force possible. The field of gravity cannot be seen or heard, yet the force is undeniable. The human body is a physical manifestation of the force that is our soul. Thus, Krishna's use of the word field is the way a physicist would use the word "field." The physical body is a field, which is the manifestation of the forces of mind, intellect, ego and spirit. The strongest force in this field is the force of will power or *Sankalpa Shakti.* It is specifically called out in the *Geeta* as one of the most powerful forces a human being is endowed with.

There is also a biological interpretation possible. The root word of *ksetra* is *ksi*, which means something that decays and undergoes constant change. The human body, the field, is made up of cells that are constantly dying and being replaced by new ones. Our method of healing is through new cells replacing old ones. There is constant change, and change is necessary for growth, new ideas, modifications, adaptations, learning and all the activities that make us individual beings. Yet with change, the body or the force remains uniquely identifiable and individual. Death of an individual cell means life for the next one. Death of an individual body means life for another. A body is not destroyed when an individual cell dies. The force, of which the body is a manifestation, is not destroyed when the body is gone. Thus, there is one life force in all bodies and that life force is God. So there is only one God and yet it resides in each body. Krishna calls himself the *Kshetrajna* (knower) in all the *kshetras* (fields).

An ability to detach one's true self, this inner force, from the interplay of the body, mind, intellect, ego, the physical breath, the passions, and the sensory organs is the objective of the path of knowledge. It is in this belief that the *Geeta* is rooted, with non-attachment considered a necessary companion for traversal on this path.

Thus, in the *Geeta*, as in science and in nature, there is no distinction between mind and matter. It is all part of evolution of the oneness of the universe.

Devotion as the Path to Knowledge

Knowing the field means knowing all this. If you know this, you are the knower of the field; you are knowledgeable. The characteristics of one who is knowledgeable are:

- absence of egoism
- draws strength in humility and lack of pride
- absence of deceit
- freedom from hypocrisy
- straightforward and pure of mind and body
- maintains a dispassion towards the objects of senses
- awareness of the deficiencies inherent in the change that is birth and death
- endurance of the pain that is old age and disease
- freedom from involvement with the self and its bondage to birth
- freedom from the desire of possession and drawing identity from man or wife, child, household
- able to calmly encounter the painful or the pleasant

- self-control through detachment
- constant balance of mind both in favorable and unfavorable circumstances

This is a daunting list. To be knowledgeable all the time is difficult or impossible. That is why in seeking knowledge, the journey itself is positioned as important. An unflinching devotion to the pursuit of knowledge, to God, can provide a focus and strengthen the will. Thus, devotion to God, in a higher being, is acceptable and even commendable for a person on the journey of self-discovery.

In this context, God is the personification of all the opposites. It is neither a being (*sat*) nor a non-being (*asat*). It is everywhere and nowhere. It is the perceiver of all senses and yet has no senses. It is within and without all human beings and constitutes both animate and inanimate creation. It is incomprehensible yet easily understood. It is at hand yet it is far away. Though indivisible (like ether) it stands as if divided among humans. It is a sustainer, creator and destroyer of humans and all knowable substance. The light of all lights, it is beyond the darkness of *maya*. God is knowledge itself; God is also the object of knowledge and devotion is the path of knowledge.

Happiness and Barriers to Happiness

The source of happiness is not in external things but within. The three elements of *sattva, rajas* and *tamas* result in different forms of happiness. Knowledge of the self is the enduring happiness. It comes from long practice and is an end of pain. Happiness can appear to be like poison in the beginning but is an elixir in the end, because it requires arduous work, renunciation of worldly goods, meditation and concentration to turn it into nectar. Happiness characterized by *sattva,* does not, like sensuous enjoyment, produce an immediate result. *Rajasic* happiness, which arises from the contact of senses with the objects, is immediate, fleeting and is like nectar at first that turns into poison in the end. *Tamasic* happiness, born of ignorance and delusion, brought by sloth, sleep, indulgence and negligence deludes the self in the beginning and in the end is a poison that slowly destroys the knowledge of the self. Self-knowledge removes from the mind the impurity of *rajas* and *tamas,* and endows it with serenity and clarity and lasting happiness.

Several metaphors are enlisted by Krishna to help Arjun understand these apparently contradictory concepts. Arjuna wants to know: how can something that makes us happy, even if fleetingly, be bad? What is the source of evil if God resides within us and we are all good?

Desire, which leads to selfishness and ignorance, which then leads to sloth and laziness, is the enemy that reside within us and clouds the ability to judge between good and evil. These are the fortresses of the enemy that we must avoid getting trapped in. The forces that propel us towards these traps, ignorance, selfishness and laziness, can be fought through self-discipline and knowledge.

Knowledge is the core that is surrounded by a fire of desire. Gratifying the senses is providing fuel to the fire, which makes it grow. As it grows bigger it needs more fuel and will consume everything in its path. One can learn to stop feeding this fire and extinguish it before it consumes the core of knowledge. A wise person learns soon that desire is evil and does not wait for the result to learn his lesson. He can teach himself to keep the senses tamed through discipline and moderation. Since all opposites reside within us, the key to taming the senses is moderation. Gluttony is as much a sin as starvation, sloth is as much a sin as being overzealous. Passion and hate, pride and self-abasement are all equally large barriers to lasting happiness.

Happiness is a daily decision.

Make it your choice. Happiness is not dependent on your

bank balance, your relationships or your circumstances. And, happiness is not a *when*—happiness is a *now*.

Happiness traps: The most common trap is to make it a future state or a past problem. The two examples are:

A—we postpone the decision—e.g. I will be happy when …(get married, buy house, take vacation..)

B—we regret the past—e.g. if such and so had not happened I could be happy now.. or if I had known it was going to get worse I would have been happy with what I had…

People will make excuses: "…if my job was easier, less repetitious, I'd be happy." Or my job was too easy and boring so I could not be happy. My son is difficult to talk to so I get stressed. The secret to handling any situation is not to change the situation but to change your attitude, and the key to happiness is not that you never get upset, frustrated or irritated—it is how quickly you decide to snap out of it.

Everything has ups and downs. Serenity is required for handling both. Successful people realize that they must learn as they go and constantly keep correcting course. The systems we humans build do it—a ship has a course and it must constantly monitor and correct. Rockets do it. Missiles do it. Why not people? Why do we need excuses?

Abstract concepts are sometimes difficult to internalize. Along with metaphors, the most common form of conveying values is through story telling—as indeed the great epics are the greatest stories as well as philosophies. Some of my favorite childhood stories seem relevant.

On Happiness: The Story of Two Cats

A big cat saw a little cat chasing its tail and asked, "Why are you chasing your tail so?"

Said the kitten, "I have learned that the best thing for a cat is happiness and that happiness is in my tail. Therefore I am chasing it and when I catch it, I shall have happiness."

Said the old cat, "My child, I too have paid attention to the problems of the universe. I too have judged that happiness is in my tail. But I have noticed that whenever I chase it, it runs away from me and when I go about my business, it just seems to come after me wherever I go."

On Knowledge: The Story of the Teacup

A man worked very diligently and acquired much prosperity and power. Feeling in need of respect he gave much to charity and engaged in social welfare. Yet he felt incomplete and betrayed by God, for had he not done all that was required of him? What more could he do? Being a man of action he decided to visit the famous Buddhist monk who resided far away in the mountains. The man enlisted his fastest jet and his entourage and went to visit the monk in his humble abode.

The monk welcomed him with a big smile.

"Please be seated," he said and pointed to a mat on the floor.

"I know why you are here but first would you like a cup of tea?"

The man reigned in his impatience, sat down and said, "Yes, I would love a cup of tea."

The monk handed him a teacup and started pouring tea into the cup from a teapot. Soon the cup was half full, then full and then it started to overflow. But the monk kept pouring.

After a while the man lost his patience and snapped, "The cup is already full. Please stop."

The monk looked at him, smiled and kept pouring and pouring and soon the teapot was empty.

"Why did you do that?" asked the man and the monk replied, "Even a full teapot cannot add tea to a cup that is full. How can I help you if you think your cup of knowledge is already full?"

On Self Empowerment: Story of the Shirt

Once upon a time, there lived a king who was just and wise. His kingdom prospered and his subjects became loyal to him. His wealth and power grew. Then the king became very sick. He called many doctors who could find nothing wrong with him so they prescribed diet and exercise. Priests and pundits were called who could find nothing wrong with him and so they prescribed charity and good works. Then an old man who was very wise came to see the king and told him that if he was to wear the shirt of a happy man his illness would vanish and he would be well again. His ministers were ordered to bring him the shirt of a happy man. Everyone was surprised, because they thought being so wealthy and powerful, the king must be the happiest man himself.

Now where to find a really happy man? The king's ministers walked around and saw a house that looked clean and tidy with children playing outside. A man with such a nice family must be happy, so they knocked on his door, explained their mission and asked for his shirt. The man replied, "I am not really happy, I have responsibilities and needs. I must work to feed my family. Go find a rich man." The king's ministers looked around and saw a party where the host was very rich. They asked the man for his shirt and explained the reason. The man said, "Who told you I am happy? See that man next door, he has far more money than I do and he is much happier. Go to him." This went on for a while. Then one day the ministers saw a man who was sitting on a rock near the riverbank. He looked peaceful and happy, so they decided to walk up to him and ask him for his shirt. "Are you happy?" they asked him. "Why, do you have doubts?" The man looked up at them and smiled. "Do you not expect any sorrow?" they queried him. "Sorrow cannot hurt me," he replied. "Then give us your shirt," the ministers said. "Shirt? What is a shirt? I do not have one to give you." The ministers realized he was not wearing a shirt. They understood. They explained the King's dilemma and thanked the man for helping them understand that the king's malady arose not from this or that physical ailment but from the erroneous notion that he was sick and unhappy. By his example the man had shown them that happiness and sorrow come only from within oneself and that a man who knows this has no need to seek objects outside himself in order to be happy.

The ministers relayed their experience to the king and he became well again.

PART III
The Seven Principles

Integrating The Concepts Of Dharma, Yoga, And Jnana

> "He who is equal in regard to well-wisher, friend
> and enemy, to the indifferent, the mediator and
> the jealous,
> also to the kinsmen, sinners and saints,
> he excels, he stands supreme" (VI:9)

In an oversimplified interpretation, *Geeta* says, to be born is to be in conflict. Good decisions in the face of conflict will lead to excellence in actions, which may lead us to an escape from the cycle of birth and death and the attainment of everlasting peace. The *Geeta* says that if we are born, we act. To be is to act. So action is our duty, a consequence of birth. One path to *nirvana*, the ultimate goal of escaping this cycle of birth and death, is through excellence in our actions. Excellence requires total discipline of our body and intellect, so that we may exercise good judgment, and make the right decisions. This will allow us to have a clear conscience, and will strengthen us in action as well as provide endurance through the tough times, giving us fortitude to endure and follow through with the choices we make. Even making no decision is an act, a choice, albeit an unconscious one. So we might as well be proactive rather than reactive. Having proposed a philosophy based around action and discipline, the *Geeta* outlines a procedure, using the metaphor of war to symbolize internal human conflict, by which one may choose the right action and the way one can best execute it.

Seven Principles

1. **Duty or Truth**—Dharma: None of us lives in isolation. We have a duty to ourselves, to society and to nature to live a good life. A good life means a life ruled by virtues of compassion, moderation and love for mankind. This should be a guiding principle in deciding the actions that we take.
2. **Non-Attachment:** Attachments of any form lead to lack of control over our body or mind, hence poor judgment and lack of focus in execution results. One must be constantly vigilant against them. Love for one can cloud our judgment just as much as hatred for another. Not only that, attachment to results causes us to worry—a complete waste of energy. If we attach ourselves to the result of action such as success, we deflect energy that would be used in performing the action into worrying about whether we would be successful or not. So detach yourself from the results. Practice non-attachment.
3. **Yoga of Knowledge:** Knowing about non-attachment is easier said than done. To be human is to be driven by our senses and our passions. So always keep an open mind and seek answers and seek the whole truth. Practice humility, as only then will your mind be open to receive answers. Seek knowledge.
4. **Yoga of Discipline:** Knowledge does not come easily either. To do that, exercise discipline first of the body and then of the mind. Practice *Yoga*. Practice moderation. Learn to discipline your body and mind through exercise

and meditation, and practice moderation in your physical needs. Sleeping too much is just as bad as sleeping too little. Overeating is as much an abuse as not eating enough. Being proud and arrogant is just as bad as having low self-esteem and groveling. Learn to recognize and conquer all extremes in your behavior.

5. **Action—*Karmayoga*:** People must work. Sages may find nirvana in meditation and a few spiritual souls may find devotion to God as the path to freedom, but for the greatest number of people work is the path to salvation. It may not always be clear what the action is or should be or even if inaction is the right form of action, but figure it out and do your best. Negligence through sloth is not an option for the *karamayogi*. Within the framework of our duty, guided by knowledge, firm in discipline, we must act.
6. **Context:** Decisions and actions are rooted within the larger context of the universe or *brahamanda* but an absolute condition only exists over the entire concept of space (i.e. space-less); the entire period of time (i.e. timeless) and the entire set of beings (a rock is the same as a person, both creations of God) that populate this time space continuum. Therefore, individual decisions must be made in the context of *dharma*, as one cannot know the absolute condition. Hence, there is no absolute right or wrong decision without the context it must be made in. In Arjuna's case the context is the war he must fight because he is a soldier, a leader. That is why, in addition to our duty dictated by our profession and our birth, we are given the context of time in the several stages we go through in life from birth to death (child—be a survivor; youth—be a learner; householder—be a provider; elder—seek non-attachment).
7. **Yoga of Devotion:** Even with all of this, there will be much conflict apparent because that is the nature of this cycle of birth and death. Contemplating this too much and

> seeking to directly correlate your action to a result is a form of pride. Give it up. It will lead you astray from the path of excellence in your action. To feel empowered and strong, believe in a higher self of whom you are a part but not the whole. While your actions appear to be driven by you, believe that an external force drives them so that while your duty is to act you are also just an instrument of a higher being. Thus, you have neither the right to any benefit nor any loss from the action. Practice devotion so that you may absolve yourself from feelings of guilt or righteousness that may result from your actions.

With all the emphasis on non-attachment and not having any rights to the fruit of the actions, the *Geeta* places the greatest emphasis on excellence in execution of individual decisions. In fact, what is abundantly clear is that the key concepts are developed so that one may achieve excellence. Thus non-attachment, knowledge, discipline and devotion are not the desired end states; rather they are the means to the goal of achieving excellence. Duty or *dharma* is the framework for making decisions and devotion or *bhakti* is the spiritual cleansing for conflict resolution. Service to others is the only goal that the *Geeta* allows us to attach ourselves to because in doing that we can do our best and still make an excellent choice. Excelling is the path to escape the cycle of birth and death.

A myriad of interpretations of the *Geeta* are possible. This particular aspect may sometimes be less emphasized in spiritual and religious interpretations of the *Geeta,* but for a practical person it is the most important aspect of the discourse. To me, this pragmatism is what provides the enduring allure of the philosophy, making it universally applicable. It is suitable in the diverse situations encountered in nature. Additionally, there is the element of timelessness in its relevancy. As long as human beings continue to be humans, focusing on action with the goal of doing the job as well as it can be done will take the focus away from conflict and lead to personal harmony.

Thus, we find the ancient wisdom of focusing on the universality of human nature and placing it in the context of the universe is applicable today just as it was in the past, despite all the changes wrought by technology and politics.

How to Apply the Key Concepts to Conflict Resolution

The 700 verses of the *Geeta* are devoted to helping Arjuna make one decision—should he fight or lay down his arms? As night begins, Arjuna is seriously considering laying down his arms and seeking death as salvation. By morning, he has decided to fight and lead his army into battle. The battlefield and the battle are metaphors for human beings and the struggle of life. As humans, we struggle with the fact that life is a choice with no predefined answers and the fact that each of us must make an individual choice in the context of the whole of the universe.

Thus, when Arjuna asks Krishna:

"Why do you encourage me to do this act of violence; kill my brothers and my teachers?"

Krishna does not condone violence. Instead he identifies Arjuna's real enemy as his desire, due to attachment. He identifies pride as another enemy in believing that his actions are solely responsible for the death of another human. Thus, he identifies Arjuna's motive for inaction to be just as impure as his motive for action. He says desire is an enemy that can be overcome by arming oneself with discipline and acting to transcend the limiting and narrow view resulting from pride and attachment. Arjuna must see beyond the conflict so that he can be strong in his actions.

While fundamentally same, human beings are not born identical. There are many different temperaments and constitutions, and within that context people may find themselves at different stages of physical and spiritual development. So, it is perfectly natural to find teachings that help people recognize and identify their individual state and find actions suited to their needs. This is done by elucidation of the three attributes of life: *gunas*. The psychological states of human beings are linked up with the spiritual quest of man through the concept of oneness with nature or *Prakriti*. Identification of humans as an element of nature provides a larger context for "I." The three qualities (*gunas*) that constitute Nature (*Prakriti*) are lucidity or truth (*sattva*), passion or senses (*rajas*) and ignorance or dark inertia (*tamas*). All these qualities together make up the nature of each individual and the universe. To be born is to have these in oneself; however, *sattva* is the highest *guna* and in as much as that quality prevails in human beings they can achieve excellence.

Conflict resolution requires spiritual discipline. The aim of spiritual discipline is to overcome ignorance and inertia through activity. Activity, *karma yoga*, is a state of learning leading to a higher state that is selfless and brings wisdom, harmony and peace. In this enlightened state, the aim is to practice devotion so as to overcome attachment to action itself. Such stoicism may seem extreme till we realize that humans are not expected to be in either extreme for long. One hopes that *rajas* completely dominates *tamas* and is guided by *sattva*.

> "For the sage ascending the hill of *Yoga*, action is the cause; for the same sage when he has got to the top of *Yoga*, self mastery is the cause" (VI:3)

Setting Goals

Context setting is important in developing goals. Developing a clear, articulated goal even if it needs modification while making a decision, can help in action planning and prioritizing conflicting demands. It is somewhat of an art to develop the goal in the right context so as to make it meaningful as well as useful in providing guidance when making a choice.

Notice that the critical drivers in decision making are:

1. Business or financial
2. Personal, family, friend or relationships
3. Societal

These often are the source of conflict and the decision needs to be a balancing act to trade off perceived gains and losses measured by the above parameters. In articulating a meaningful goal, we must involve the heart and the mind to get our own commitment to excel in the action. If we enlist one to the exclusion of the other we will not be able to summon our biggest asset in difficult times; our will power (*Sankalp Shakti*).

How to Overcome Self Defeating Behaviors

Thinking and feeling are the assets that have allowed the human species to survive and dominate all others (some unfortunately to extinction). So it goes without saying that they are here to stay and are common across culture, race and religion and are finely tuned to support us in life preservation and enhancing the quality of life. However, when applied in excessive measure, without the balance needed for individual gain as well as societal gain, they can cause an individual to indulge in self defeating behavior. This is consistent with the classification of the *gunas (sattava, rajas and tamas)* as explained in the *Geeta.*

Individuals tend to form groups and certain patterns in group living get established that cut across cultures and societies. Families, clans, neighborhoods, societies, common interest groups are found all across the globe. This suggests that there are characteristics preprogrammed into human nature that have an implication on group dynamics. Thus there are implications for an individual when creating the best group environment. To ensure success in the goal we must be able to enlist the best human behavior from all involved in a group. To get the best behavior from others, *Geeta* says you must first control your own behavior. When that does not come naturally such as in the case of a conflict, learn to recognize your self defeating behavior and correct it before it affects others and causes them to make similar mistakes.

The following is list of behavioral traps and outlines a procedure for understanding the trap and proposes an action oriented approach to modifying one's behavior.

I. Behavioral Trap: Emotions before Reason

Emotion is the first screen for all information received. Hidden agendas develop.

Why We Do It:

1. Bad news is heard first and loudest; even anticipated where none was intended – it is a mode of emotional self preservation.
2. In communications, emotion is conveyed first even to the extent of obscuring facts because it makes us feel better.

What to Do:

1. Acknowledge the emotion and take the time to heal before doing anything that will make you react deceitfully or overly emotionally.
2. Make a list of what is bothering you. You cannot balance positive and negative messages but you can balance the emotions they may generate and this action will help moderate emotions.
3. Seek clarification; communication of negative situation is not a negative reflection of you as a person.

II. Behavioral Trap: Loss Aversion except When Threatened

We avoid risky situations when feeling secure but fight frantically when threatened – both can be inappropriate.

Why We Do It:

1. People resist change except when they are dissatisfied.
2. We are afraid of the unknown and assume a loss will be incurred.

What to Do:

1. Find a place or relationship where you can be safe to think about or discuss the change and how it impacts you.
2. If you want people to support change, frame the current situation as threatening but the new one as safe.

III. Behavioral Trap: Confidence before Realism

Feel more self-confident than reality justifies. Appears overbearing to others or you may come across as one who does not listen.

Why We Do It:

1. It's a way to avoid pre-work.
2. It's a way to maintain dignity when threatened.

What to Do:

1. Understand that important clues could have been missed and be prepared for the unknown or unpredicted.
2. Be flexible in your plans. Understand that you had no safety margin planned for the impact from random events.
3. Routinely ask open ended questions about possible difficulties in accomplishing goal related challenges.
4. Accept differing viewpoints gracefully and know that you will not be right all the time. Openly acknowledge.

IV. Behavioral Trap: Classification before Analysis

Tendency to quickly classify people, experience or situations into categories - good/bad or in/out – rather than engage in seemingly time consuming analysis

Why We Do It:

1. People of diverse backgrounds do not automatically mix–stereotyping occurs.
2. Subgroups develop generating competitive rather than collaborative behavior.

What to Do:

1. Spend extra time and effort to overcome this deep rooted human propensity. Realize that the gain will have a longer term payback.
2. Meet regularly. Establish processes with built in controls to ensure objectivity.

V. Behavioral Trap: Herding Instinct

Gossip, empathy and mind reading (often erroneously)

Why We Do It:

1. People bond by sharing information; especially when anticipating power shifts and to form a safety group.
2. When no information is available we create it.

What to Do:

1. Communicate often and regularly even if only to say no new information.
2. Keep tabs on the rumor mill and make sure it stays healthy; not malicious.
3. Manage communications by informal means; talk to people.

VI. Behavioral Trap: Contest and Display

Engaging in win/lose competitions and one-upmanship.

Why We Do It:

1. Competition may get people more mobilized than a call for collaboration even when that is more beneficial in the long term.

What to Do:

1. Encourage rationality while understanding this behavior.
2. Reward collaboration over competition; engage in group recognition.
3. Frame and then frequently remind people of common goals- how the group is more effective as a team.

VII. Behavioral Trap: Hierarchy and Power

Expect to lead or influence others by showing status rather than capability.

Why We Do It:

People find comfort in distinct roles and responsibilities but do not respond with a positive emotion to domination.

What to Do:

1. Understand that everybody needs to have status and assert their individuality. Allow others to show status first.
2. Create an environment where there are many ways to achieve status.
3. Understand that desire to obtain status is natural in a group and you cannot win long term if others lose short term.
4. Do not expect them to thank you for your charity if their status is lower than yours in their eyes.

PART IV
Empowering yourself

Practical Do's and Don't's

"The greatness is not what we do, but unavoidably it is always in how we do, what we do."
—Swami Chinmayananda

Take all the philosophy and psychology of the *Geeta* and boil it down to its essence and we end up with some very practical tips. World philosophers and spiritual leaders of today and yesterday teach tips that are not very different from what the *Geeta* sets forth.

"Happiness is an expression of the soul in considered actions."—Aristotle in 4th century BC

That says an individual must make thoughtful decisions and follow up with appropriate action to be happy. After all, what do we all want from life? Happiness. What do we all have? Soul. What can we all do? Make decisions and act with excellence.

A bottom line oriented retelling could be: work hard and smart and you'll be happy.

The skeptic in us may ask—is that so?

Introducing the concept of others, Aristotle says "*In the arena of human life the honors and rewards fall to those who show their good qualities in action,*" thus integrating the individual into society, for we do not exist alone in this world. We must live in harmony, not only with ourselves but also with our surroundings. Some examples of good qualities may be judgment, compassion and diligence. Good judgment resulting in considered actions done with compassion, followed by hard work, sounds like a nice way to define excellence or "eminently good." Since these are individual attributes, we are reminded that it is our responsibility and our choice to excel, for which the internal reward is happiness and the external reward is success.

By adding the personal and societal dimensions and adding an external measure of happiness, Aristotle makes the skeptic in us think harder, hopefully hard enough to realize that thinking alone will not provide all answers. We must also enlist the heart.

Arguably, no single volume of text has embodied this aspect of blending reason and emotion more forcefully and emphatically than the *Bhagavad Geeta.* Additionally, what I like about the *Geeta* is that it squarely places the responsibility on the individual to choose action over inaction, duty over self, knowledge over ignorance, morality over selfishness, humility over ego and a universal love over fleeting emotion. The motivational carrot it offers the person, who chooses well, is *nirvana*—escape from this cycle of birth and death where we must deal with such conflicts.

"*A thought which does not result in an action is nothing much, and an action which does not proceed from a thought is nothing at all.*"—Georges Bernanos, 1955

Action undertaken after careful consideration of various options, guided by moral considerations, makes you believe in yourself, which in turn, gives you the emotional strength to overcome obstacles encountered in the course of action.

Hence, the ability to choose well, and make sound decisions, is the key skill in business as well as in life outside the workplace. "A thinking animal, such is man." The ability to learn and think also means there is no prescribed formula for anyone to follow in life. We make our own choices. We live as individuals in the context of society and in relationship to others. That means change is a constant force internally and externally. Not being a linear process of cause and effect but more of a jumble of everything happening at once, we are always in a state of making a decision for ourselves or being affected by another's decision. Simply speaking, you have to take sides. If you choose not to, you will find yourself aligned on one side or another based on someone else's decision. Sometimes that may be what you desire, other times it may not. You can choose to be in control of your actions. If not, others will drive your action.

Reason versus Emotion

Reason and emotion are the two forces that drive decision-making. A combination of the two is needed for good decisions. Born in 1623, Blaise Pascal, mathematician and philosopher extraordinaire, classified the two extremes of reason and emotion, in which one dominates to the exclusion of the other as "skepticism" or "dogmatism." Neither is desirable. Pure reason can lead to a state of skepticism when the contradictions of the universe make no sense. As for dogmatists, they base their reasoning on non-existent foundations. "Reason's final step is the recognition that there are an infinite number of things beyond it; it is merely feeble if it does not go as far as to grasp that." Powerful reason becomes conscious of its limitations when it reaches them.

Pascal's logic-driven theory predicts that pushed to extreme limits, skepticism and dogmatism would lead to a complete paralysis of thought and action. Nothing will make sense. The duality of the universe, nature versus nurture, biology versus culture, personal versus societal, mind versus body will always appear to be in conflict. The only way out is to understand and accept this as part of a greater truth, make decisions and choices you can believe in and allow them to become your guiding principles.

According to Pascal "We come to know truth not only by reason, but even more by our heart... It is just as useless for reason to demand of the heart proofs of its first principles in order to concur in them, as it would be for the heart to demand of reason an intuitive knowledge of all its propositions before accepting them."

One can derive from this that decision making is not a linear, precise, mathematical process. It is complex, ambiguous and often, a compromise of reason and emotion. Having a philosophical understanding of the universe, the fact that it has a time span far greater than a human beings', our role for the short time that we live in it, can be a way to reduce tension and conflict.

Intellect and heart, reason and emotion, together, will provide you all the information and intuition you need to lead your life. It is up to you to decide how you will do it. Consider this image :

> "....the soul as lord of the chariot which is the body, with the intellect as the charioteer and mind as the reins. The senses are the horses and they range over many paths, but are brought under control by the good charioteer who has understanding and a restrained mind." (Geoffrey Parrinder in *Upanishads, Gita and Bible*)

Excellence versus Perfection

People often confuse perfection with excellence. To be born is to be imperfect. Nature is not perfect; life is not perfect; I am not even sure perfection is a goal for us humans.

I recently read a story that really helped me understand this. The story is about a baseball player who was so perfect that when he pitched, the batter was out in the first pitch. When he was at bat, nobody could get him out. So what was the result? Nobody could play with him. Life is like a ballgame; it works best when all the players do the very best job they can, learn from their mistakes and then when it's all over go on to play the next game better than they did before. To me that defines excellence and it is what we should strive for.

I like this story because a fear of not achieving perfection at something keeps people from even trying things. If you don't try it, you can't get better at it; you can't excel.

Excellence is achievable; perfection is not.

According to Hindu philosophy, when we get so excellent at what we do that we are perfect, we will achieve *nirvana* and escape from this cycle of birth and death.

Decisions versus Strategy

In the context of war, the meaning of the word "strategy" is easy to understand—it is a decision of really big scope. In war there is always controversy and success is not guaranteed. Risk is inherent to war and risk is inherent to a strategy. Alexander defeated the massive, well-rested army of King Porus by mounting a dual attack on the enemy, using his tired and hungry soldiers, who had trekked over inhospitable terrain for months. A small army of his soldiers attacked as expected from the front while a larger army trekked over more mountains and more inhospitable terrain, to mount a simultaneous unexpected attack from the rear. His strategy was to utilize the strength and complacency of Porus against him and to use the element of surprise in the attack. His decision to split his troops, further reducing their numbers, was risky but it paid off. At the time it was made, the wisdom of this decision was not obvious. The dubious value of the surprise element was being offset by the certainty of hardships in further trekking across impassable terrain. However, Alexander acknowledged this but felt he had only one winning strategy. The risk was understood and communicated to the generals and to the army so a coordinated attack could be mounted. Using this example, the relationship between strategy and decision may be based around scope. Given that a large scope decision will drive several smaller decisions made by several different people to attain the same goal, communication of the logic or reasoning behind a particular decision or strategy becomes a critical skill also.

I versus You: Relate to Others

Decisions are made in a context and an environment. No decision is independent of its environment and a critical component of environment is other people. No decision can have a successful outcome if it does not consider people. So it is imperative for a good decision-maker to develop skills that enhance the understanding of human behavior and think of the decision not from an individual but from a group perspective. This requires a shift of focus from the personal to the environmental.

Data gathering is one tool for shifting the focus from oneself to others. By getting inputs from a variety of sources, one puts the decision in the context of its environment. Thinking about people affected or involved with the decision is the step when you complete this transfer of energy from yourself to others and the environment. When you begin to think of the whole ecosystem and not just an individual, the result will be that the decision and actions are viewed and owned by others also. This greatly enhances the chances of a successful outcome from the decision.

Whether you want to build a bridge, win a war or throw a great party, it is the people who will make it happen. While this is an old truism, today's "knowledge economy" has turned it into the single most critical success factor for an individual as well as an organization. Add this to the fact that in a global business, environmental isolation is impossible and free and rapid movement of information is possible. Only people generate ideas, apply data to problems and create knowledge. One quickly realizes the importance of having, retaining and utilizing the best minds in a company. No more can an organization afford to ignore the "softer skills" of management. People and human resource issues are no longer to be relegated to a lowly status and to be the playground of personnel departments.

Fortunately this is not at odds with what our goal is; it is just a realization that excellence in decision-making is not a solitary occupation. More than ever, we must see the big picture, see the whole and its individual parts, thinking creatively and with empathy. Good decisions and successful outcomes cannot be achieved without support from others.

Cherish people and relationships much more than your most valuable asset. Though we think we are eager to treat people as special, in practice we often overlook their needs. It is a natural mistake because people will generally recover from our neglect, whereas our cherished physical asset may not. But an asset can be replaced while relationships get wounded. Wounds leave scars. What takes a long time to build, such as trust, individual relationships or group dynamics, can be destroyed very quickly and can then take a very long time to rebuild if that can be done at all. Compared to that, physical assets can be replaced relatively quickly.

In honing your decision-making skills, take the long-term view. Understand people. Understand their emotional and intellectual needs, motivation, drives, values, and limitations. But above all have empathy and never be judgmental of a person. Judging a person is very different from judging their actions and behaviors. The latter are fair game and as a manager or leader may even be a responsibility that when carried out with empathy and understanding will even be appreciated. The former is not.

Understand Human Nature

If you understand human nature and internalize the fact that all people are the same species, you will be non-judgmental. This will show in all your behaviors. You will know that you mirror every deficiency you see in the person standing in front of you. And you will have compassion. Compassion brings you trust.

A lesson in evolutionary psychology can be particularly helpful in enhancing our understanding of people and their motivations. While technology is advancing at supersonic and breakneck speeds, our physical and emotional makeup is programmed to move at the speed of genetic mutation. Even glaciers are moving fast when you think about how much humans have changed since they first evolved. So when it comes to people, slow down and remember you are of the same species. And leverage that knowledge. Do not let minor differences of color, race and culture cloud your thinking in today's diverse environment when you need creativity and originality of thought more than ever.

Homo sapiens emerged 200,000 years ago, and people still exhibit those traits that made survival possible then: fighting furiously when threatened, trading information, sharing secrets and propagating clan living. So while the world around us has changed we have not. This does not mean people are all alike underneath. But it helps to understand what has contributed to our survival for so long and how it impacts the workplace. Understanding leads to an assessment about how much to fight and suppress or enlist what we are genetically programmed to do.

Framing: Understanding Decision Frames

Each one of us is conditioned to view life and form opinions based on who we are from birth, how we are brought up, our position in society and our circumstances. So you might say that one goes through life with a frame around one's face. When I look at you what I see depends on how narrow, wide, angular, or colored my frame is. As soon as I realize this, I can consciously try to get my head out of this default frame. I can try to broaden my frame. I can understand that this invisible frame dictates certain constraints on how I see things, which may or may not be the same as those of someone else. If I can understand this about myself then I can understand this about you. I can also understand that if you and I have had dissimilar upbringing we may be looking at the same situation or the same person and yet not perceive the same thing. As soon as I understand this, a dialog is possible for us to resolve the differences we see. As soon as a dialog is possible we can both understand one another's point of view. After that one can choose to broaden one's frame, change a point of view or reaffirm a point of view, but in all cases it is a richer and more sympathetic understanding of oneself and one's fellow being. There is less apparent conflict in our differing views and potential decision. The modern concept of frames is taken as a given in the *Geeta*. Everyone is born to have his or her own individual *dharma* or duty.

This natural frame helps us deal with complexity and conflict. The same framing technique can be used for decision making. Just as each one of us walks about with a frame to help simplify, we also have the capacity to make decisions by framing the decision around factors that are the most important. While personal frames get built unconsciously and we must cultivate the ability to get out of the frame if needed, decision frames must be actively constructed to simplify and help make a choice in the face of conflict or inaction. Important factors go inside the frame while the rest go outside.

The analogy of a frame is also useful in understanding how two different persons may view the same scene and come away with two completely different perceptions of the "reality" and similarly, how a person may come to different decisions depending on what he or she perceives the situation to be.

Barrier to Understanding Others: Emotional Traps

If you understand yourself, you can understand others. But there is no limit to self-delusion once you get started. We all do it because it is our built-in escape mechanism for dealing with the harsh realities of life. Accept that you will do it periodically but then act and stop.

You can start by asking yourself at the end of everyday—Did I do what I chose to do?

If the answer is yes, sleep easy.

If not, start asking yourself—Why? Invariably, the answer is one that places the responsibility for your action on someone else. This is how you escape taking responsibility for yourself and why these behaviors get in the way of your understanding others.

To instill self-discipline in this process, do a five-minute retrospective every night. Keep asking yourself the primary question—Did I do what I chose to do today?—till the answer to the question is more often yes than no.

Recognize self-defeating behaviors and emotions that get in the way of success and stop indulging in them.

Emotional traps outlined below are a form of wasted energy- energy that can be utilized in other, more effective ways. They also keep you fixated in your own emotional state and do not allow you to understand others or get factual data that you can act on.

I. Emotional Trap: Guilt and Worry

They give you an excuse for inaction by focusing energy to yourself instead of the other person.

These are emotional outlets that cause paralysis in the present moment.

Why We Do It:

1. Guilt allows you to focus on past deeds and Worry about

the future, thus allowing escape from the present actions required.

2. These are self-serving false notions where we believe we worry about people we love. "If I worry about you, it shows I care and that somehow makes it all right that I don't really have to do anything for you."
3. Guilt means we wish to reform ourselves so we can escape taking responsibility for past actions. "I am really an OK person because I am suffering too and hence, I don't need to do anything. Instead of becoming a giver, I can be a taker—of your sympathy."

Actions to Avoid Trap:

1. Make a list of the items causing you worry and another one for guilt.
2. Append actions that you did that are the cause of your guilt feeling to the list. Do the same for the worry list, except in this case they may not be your actions.
3. Seek information from a variety of people to validate or invalidate your perspective. This action itself will help to get you out of the paralysis mode.
4. List actions you can take to reduce your feelings of guilt/ worry.
5. Do something at the personal, social or societal level depending on what you are worrying about and what your capacity is.
6. Don't worry about world hunger; donate time or money to a charitable cause.

II. Emotional Trap: Anger and Blame

Cause wasted energy in seeking justice.

Why We Do It:

1. To justify maintaining the current situation while shifting responsibility.

2. To perpetuate the past decisions even if we know them to be mistakes.

Actions to Avoid Trap:

1. Remind yourself of the objectives—why you started on this to begin with.
2. Propose several alternatives and make a conscious effort to list advantages/disadvantages.
3. Remember you are planning. The status quo gets older and less desirable with time.

III. Emotional Trap: Regret or Exultation

Cause paralysis in the present moment.

Why We Do It:

1. To perpetuate the past decisions even if we know them to be mistakes or only minor wins.

Actions to Avoid Trap:

1. Seek opinions from people uninvolved with past history.
2. Do not get your ego involved. A bad result does not mean a bad decision was made.
3. Cultivate an environment where employees or others are rewarded for their decision making skills with the data at hand rather than solely on outcomes.

IV. Emotional Trap: Approval Seeking or Approval Withholding

Cause unhealthy relationships based on unsustainable emotions.

Why We Do It:

1. Seeking information in support of our bias or action while discounting opposing information or action.

Action to Avoid Trap:

1. Get someone you respect to play devil's advocate.
2. Ask open ended questions when gathering data.

3. Apply equal rigor in examining all data whether it be confirming or opposing.

V. Emotional Trap: Low Self-Esteem or High Ego

Cause avoidance in taking on responsibility for action.

Why We Do It:

1. It is a safety mechanism to keep us from being emotionally destroyed when we perceive ourselves to have failed.

Action to Avoid Trap:

1. Don't be judgmental of yourself or others.
2. Measure your success by engaging in activity and not becoming attached to the result.
3. Enjoy doing the task at hand without waiting to feel good after the task.

VI. Emotional Trap: Play Victim or Conqueror

Cause unhealthy relationships based on unsustainable emotions.

Why We Do It:

1. Allows misstating the problem so as to undermine the whole decision making process.

Action to Avoid Trap:

1. Pose the problem in a neutral fashion with some built-in redundancy.
2. Try several different frames before accepting one.
3. Evaluate the frame throughout the process against the goal

Elements of Non-Judgmental Behaviors: Verification Exercise

Understanding human behavior means empathizing with people. This can only be done if we see all humans as being one and our duty in life to be dictated by factors larger than any individual or society. This understanding and actions stemming from this awareness are not bounded by space-time considerations.

In verifying that you took a non-judgmental approach, ask yourself if in making your decisions you were:

Detached or equally attached to all involved parties?

Detached or equally attached to the possible outcomes for the different parties?

If truthfully the answer is yes, you are unbiased and are making the right decision.

To visualize an empowered person, think of what S. Radhakrishnan said in the context of describing Gandhi:

> *He who wrongs no one fears no one. He has nothing to hide and so is fearless. He looks everyone in the face. His step is firm, his body upright, and his words are direct and straight."* — S. Radhakrishnan in *Gandhi—All Men Are Brothers*

Do:

1. Be self-confident—you are the instrument of God.

2. Enlist your Will Power—It is your strongest ally in times of conflict. The power is within you.

3. Ask questions to increase your knowledge—seek counsel from others, keeping an open mind.

4. Take time to reflect before making a decision—the choice is yours, so having gathered enough data, make your own decision.

5. Make the right decision—enlist your heart and mind till you have resolved all conflict and firmly believe in the decision you have made. There is no room for ambiguity in believing in your choice.

6. Practice moderation and self discipline—Eat right, exercise the body and meditate to calm the mind. A healthy body is necessary for doing your best. It is also a prerequisite for achieving control over your mind. A fleeting mind leads to lack of focus.

7. Help others—increase your viewpoint to include others. Others doing well can make you feel just as good as doing well yourself.

8. Be calm—excess emotion is a waste of energy and can sway judgment. If you find yourself agitated, wait till you are calm and balanced before making any decisions.

Don't:

1. When faced with tough choices, don't take refuge in inaction —make decisions and follow up with action.

2. Don't be judgmental of others—it keeps you from being kind. See the failings of others as mirrors into yourself and understand that you too may need help sometime. This will impact how you behave with others.

3. Don't worry—it wastes precious energy. This can be achieved by not thinking about results.

4. Don't feel guilt—it keeps you from correcting the wrong you did. It is a negative outlet for energy.

5. Instead do something to compensate for your misbehavior. Charity is a positive channel for this energy.

6. Don't make excuses for yourself—you can overcome the lower urges and tendencies if you try. This is a constant struggle. Acknowledge that and just keep trying.

7. Don't focus on your weaknesses—this is another escape route to inaction and comes couched with self-pity.

8. Don't focus on perfection—there is no such thing on earth and it can keep you from acting by making you feel inadequate and afraid. To be born is to be imperfect. That is why the cycle of birth and death exists. Perfection only exists in Nirvana.

9. Don't be slaves to your senses—senses are for your protection but can easily overpower and control your actions. Being aware is the first step in being in control of you.

CONCLUSION

Chapter eighteen concludes the divine dialog between Arjuna and Krishna on the topic of decision making.

"Reflect on the knowledge you have gained and then act as you choose," says Krishna to Arjuna in XVIII:63.

You might ask why such a long dialogue is needed (eighteen chapters and 700 verses, no less) if at the end of it all Arjuna still has to make up his own mind. What was the point?

The *Bhagavad Geeta* essentially outlines a process for decision making. If we understand the process we can resolve inner conflict and questioning that may undermine the ability to act with excellence. The point is that when properly considered, the decision to act and go into battle is an obvious one for Arjuna. It engenders no conflict in the soul that might make Arjun deliver a sub-par performance in battle or might reduce his ability to do the best job he can do. Krishna knows that Arjun will choose to go into battle if he understands that it is his duty or *dharma.*

So, Krishna asks Arjuna if he has listened carefully. If he has, after careful consideration, he should do whatever feels right to him. At the same time he offers Arjuna complete shelter in his divine presence, saying that the right choice will come to him if he places his trust in God. Both of these concepts are important for the reader to understand. Although we feel we are making choices, our inner god actually drives us to do the right thing, so whatever we do will be right eventually.

At the beginning of chapter eighteen, Arjuna has one final question for Krishna. He asks Krishna the difference between renunciation—*tyaga*—and relinquishment—*sanyasa*. Actions should not be driven by desire. It is not what we want that should drive action. It is what is right to do that drives action and the only way to know what is right to do is to look within us with complete faith in God. This sort of "renunciation" or selflessness (*tyaga*) is the basis of action. Action is based on faith in god, we act as instruments of God and we must relinquish any right to the result of action. We neither gain from any benefit nor lose from any harm that may result from the action. Indeed we cannot know what is gain or loss as we do not know the full context of nature (*prakriti*). Therefore, we should practice humility but act with self confidence with full faith in our abilities.

It is essential that we do not confuse the philosophy of detachment from results and excessive emotion with detachment from action.

The eighteenth chapter, the *Bhagavad Geeta*, concludes with Sanjaya expressing his joy and confidence in the virtue of a world where there is a Krishna, the lord of *Yoga*, and there is Arjuna, the man of thoughtful action.

The *Geeta* chapter ends with Arjuna making the decision to go into battle and the story continues in *Mahabharata*. What follows is a detailed description of the eighteen days of bloody war replete with stories of valor, heroics, and sacrifice as well as treachery, betrayal and curmudgeonly. The war starts with good intentions on both sides. It starts in an orderly fashion with strict adherence to the rules of engagement that define a fair fight. For example a foot soldier must only fight another foot soldier and service personnel such as charioteers are not to be attacked. As war progresses and heavy losses are incurred on both sides, the scene gets uglier and more ruthless and eventually both sides resort to unfair means. The war ends with the death of all the Kauravas and the entire army of the Pandavas which includes their sons. Only the five Pandava brothers remain alive and Yudhishtir, the eldest Pandava, takes over the duty of ruling a devastated land peopled by grief stricken relatives, friends and sages. This epic tale is replete with many sub plots and stories that are not relevant to the main theme but illustrate how heroes are also humans and when their lower instincts rule they can make mistakes and do things that are wrong. Arjuna fulfills his role of supporting his brother's rule.

In keeping with the theme of seeking peace and salvation, eventually the Pandava brothers begin a journey to ascend Mount *Kailash*, abode of the Gods, symbol of heaven, to find *nirvana* or escape from this cycle of life and death, the only place where there is lasting happiness. This long journey is an interesting development in the saga as it deals with the next stage of life when managing the kingdom is not their duty. Eventually, the Kauravas and the Pandavas find themselves in heaven where there is peace and harmony amongst them with no malice for their trials on earth.

Just because the story of *Mahabharata* is centered on a major battle one must not assume that battle is glorified. Battle is a metaphor for living. My interpretation is that it seeks to provide a realistic view of what happens in life and how one may attempt to conquer one's baser instincts. According to C. V. Narasimhan in his translation of the *Mahabharata*, Yudhishtir says "In all cases, war is evil. Who that strikes is not struck in return? Victory and defeat are the same to one who is killed."

Decision Making and Action as a Process

One hopes that decision making is the conscious compromise of reason and emotion, influenced by internal and external forces where the tradeoffs and risks are understood and communicated. In reality, decisions are often made in a split second. How often have you heard about that defining moment, with much of the rationalizing and action planning done afterwards? Either way works. This is perfectly acceptable because the process of decision making is not linear, it is not prescriptive and it is subject to change based on unforeseen happenings. Thus one may argue, why bother to understand the logic that drives a decision, why understand the emotion? Why treat a complex non-linear process as if it could be sliced and diced along the axes of reason, emotion and philosophy? Why pretend that we can take a logical step by step approach when there is not a clear beginning or end to a decision?

Do it because it can be done. Understand the limitations and advantages of the process. Do it because it is a better option to be prepared than to be unprepared. Understand that preparation may not always position you optimally. Do it because it improves the odds in the game of life. Do it because there is no other better way.

Ultimately decision making is about weighing alternatives and taking responsibility for one's action. What can be more empowering than a careful evaluation of oneself and one's circumstances and then finding the power within?

Bibliography and Reference Guide

1. *Bhagavad Gita*, translated by Barbara Stoler Miller, Bantam Books, a division of Random House Inc., New York
2. The *Bhagavad Gita*, text, translation and commentary by Sri Aurobindo; Sri Aurobindo Divine Life Trust, Rajasthan
3. Lectures on *Bhagavad Gita* by Swami Paramarthananda; Published by The Samskrita Academy, Chennai
4. *Bhagavad*gita translated by Sir Edwin Arnold; Dover Publications Inc; New York
5. *The Legacy of Yoga in Bhagavad Geeta* translation and commentary by Prabha Duneja; Publisher Govindram Hasanand, Delhi
6. *Perennial Psychology of the Bhagavad Gita* by Swami Rama; Himalayan International Institute of *Yoga* Science and Philosophy of the U.S.A., Pennsylvania
7. *Geeta Pravachan* (Hindi) by Vinoba; Sarva-Seva-Sangh Prakashan; Varanasi
8. *Upanishads, Gita and Bible* : a comparative study of Hindu

and Christian Scriptures by Edward Geoffrey Parrinder; Sheldon Press

9. The *Mahabharata* translated by Chakravarthi V. Narasimhan; Columbia University Press, New York
10. *100 Great Indians Through the Ages,* H.N. Verma, Amrit Verma; GIP Books, Campbell
11. *Light on Yoga* by B. K. S. Iyengar; George Allen and Unwin ltd., Schocken Books, a division of Random House Inc., New York
12. *The Works of Blaise Pascal,* Black's Readers Service Company, Random House Inc, New York
13. *The Pocket Aristotle* Editor W. D. Ross Oxford University Press; A Washington Square Publication; Simon and Schuster, New York
14. *The Purpose of Your Life: Finding Your Place in the World Using Synchronicity, Intuition, and Uncommon Sense* by Carol Adrienne; Eagle Book, An imprint of William Morrow and Company, New York
15. *Kinds of Power: A guide to its Intelligent Uses* by James Hillman; Published by Doubleday, a division of Bantam Doubleday Dell Publishing Group, New York
16. *The 7 Habits of Highly Effective People* by Stephen R. Covey; A Fireside Book, Simon and Schuster, New York
17. *The Art of Wealth* translation and commentary by Thomas Cleary; Health Communications Inc., Florida
18. *Smart Choices* by John S. Hammond, Ralph L. Keeney, Howard Raiffa; Harvard Business Press, Massachusetts
19. *If Aristotle Ran General Motors: the New Soul of Business* by Tom Morris; Henry Holt and Company, New York
20. *How the Mind Works* by Steven Pinker; W. W. Norton and Company Inc., New York
21. *Memos for Management Leadership* by James L. Hayes; American Management Association, New York
22. *The Way of the Leader* by Donald G. Krause; Nicholas Brealey Publishing ltd., London
23. *The Tao of Personal Leadership* by Diane Dreher;

HarperBusiness, A division of Harper Collins Publishers, New York

24. *The Leadership Wisdom of Jesus: Practical Lessons for Today* by Charles C. Manz; Berrett-Koehler Publishers Inc. San Francisco
25. *The Wisdom of Wolves* by Twyman L. Towery; Published by Sourcebooks, Illinois
26. *Dealing With People You Can't Stand* by Rick Brinkman, Rick Kirschner; McGraw Hill Inc., U. S. A.
27. *How To Talk So People Listen : the Real Key to Job Success* by Sonya Hamlin; Harper and Row Publishers, New York
28. *Nudge*: Improving Decisions About Health, Wealth and Happiness by Richard H. Thaler and Cass R. Sunstein, Yale University Press, New Haven and London
29. *Karma Capitalism, Special Report on Managing* by Pete Engardio, BusinessWeek, October 30, 2006, pages 84-91

Author photo courtesy Kris Pfeifer

About the Author

Neerja Raman is an award winning executive and author in technology research and new business creation. She is a 2005 Hall of Fame inductee, Women in Technology International and has been honored by several organizations including Federation of Indo-Americans, the California State Senate and Indian-American Women Empowered.

Neerja has served on the Advisory Committee for Cyber-Infrastructure, National Science Foundation and is board member of several non-profits. Neerja is a graduate of the Kellogg Executive Program, Northwestern University, and has Masters Degrees from S.U.N.Y Stony Brook, New York and Delhi University, India.

Neerja Raman was born in India and came to the United States for graduate studies. Her first job was Research Associate at a university. She has been a Software Engineer at a startup, R&D Manager and Lab Director at Hewlett Packard and is now Senior Fellow at Stanford University where she is doing research in the field of social entrepreneurship. Throughout her career, Neerja has found that she is one of a handful of technical women, if not the only one, in situations that require making decisions that impact many lives. As such, she has developed a unique, self-reliant but compassionate leadership style based on long term thinking but rooted in action.

Neerja is a much sought after mentor and speaker. She is wife, mother, daughter, sister and a decision maker. She lives in California with her husband.

Her personal website is http: //neerja.raman-net.com.

Her blog is Digital Provide: From Good to Gold http://fromgoodtogold.blogspot.com/

CPSIA information can be obtained at www.ICGtesting.com
Printed in the USA
BVOW06s0458290716

457097BV00039B/78/P

9 781588 989543